Undivided Devotion

Spiritual Focus for Single Disciples

Undivided Devotion

Spiritual Focus
for Single Disciples

G. Steve Kinnard
EDITOR

DISCIPLESHIP
PUBLICATIONS
INTERNATIONAL

1-888-DPI-BOOK
www.dpibooks.com

Undivided Devotion

©1997 by Discipleship Publications International
One Merrill Street, Woburn, MA 01801
www.dpibooks.com

Printed in the United States of America

Cover design: Chris Costello
Interior design: Chad Crossland
ISBN 1-57782-040-1

The New York City ministry staff would like to dedicate this book to the administrators of the Aces World Sector of the International Churches of Christ who work tirelessly for the kingdom.

Contents

Being Single

Bright Lights. Big City. The Melting Pot. The Empire City. The Capital of the World. New York, New York, is know by many names. It is a city of contrasts. New York beckons people from all over the world to move there. It hypnotizes them with the call, "If I can make it there, I can make it anywhere. It's up to you—New York, New York."

This call is especially enticing for singles. Singles come to New York to study, work, party, escape life and "get their names in lights." Some find success, but many others fail. Some singles have been crushed by the big city. It's not Kansas. It is cruel, ruthless and unforgiving. It is a city filled with darkness.

The single's life in this and other cities can be lonely. It can be full of insecurity and fears. Often it is filled with the search for meaning and lasting fulfillment. This search can turn down many roads including the roads of sexual looseness, experimentation with drugs, a failing to commit to ideals and principles and a sense of drifting. These are some of the characterizations of the so-called "Generation X," a generation made up primarily of singles.

The single life does not have to be like this, however. Jesus came to "give life and give it to the full" (John 10:10). Singles committed to Jesus Christ experience life differently.

The New York City Church of Christ offers a bright ray of hope in a city of despair. In 1983 Steve and Lisa Johnson were sent by the Boston Church of Christ to plant a church in New York City. They came with eighteen people to a city of eighteen million. It was a one in a million shot. Steve and Lisa knew that a crucial part of the church in New York would be the singles' ministry. Because of their "singular" vision, one of the largest, most vibrant singles' ministries in the world has been built.

The singles' ministry stretches out across the metropolitan area of New York. It cuts across many barriers—age differences, economic barriers, racial and educational differences. It offers hope. It is a ministry that is full of vigor and vitality. Singles are drawn to it. Comments from some singles within the New York church illustrate the difference the church has made:

> One sister in Manhattan said, "Being single in the church means that I have nothing except 'time' to live life to the full and fulfill God's plans for me and New York City. It means I should have nothing to distract me from God's mission."

> A single mother living in New Jersey commented, "It takes great faith, determination and trust to believe that God knows what is best for me. I just want to be like Caleb and have a dogged trust in God."

> A brother from Manhattan mentioned that being single in the kingdom meant that he could serve God with an undivided heart.

> A sister in Manhattan commented, "Even though I'm single, Isaiah 54:5 says I have a husband—God! Just as I hope one day to make a vow of uncompromising love and faithfulness to my '/husband I'd already made that vow to my 'maker'/husband

when I became a Christian. My heart, mind and soul are committed in action to God till death do us...reunite!"

Around the world in biblical churches, singles make up a large portion of the membership. The singles' ministry is diverse and varied. The ages in a singles' ministry can range from the 20s to the 80s, and it includes students, doctors, lawyers, blue-collar workers, secretaries, nannies, teachers and various other professionals. Some singles are looking to get established, and some have been established for years. Singles may be dating, engaged, separated, divorced or widowed. Some have children that they are raising, and some have already raised their children. Some live alone, and some share apartments with several roommates. The singles' ministry is the most diverse ministry of them all. The needs are many and must be met by the leadership of the church.

Thus, this book is long overdue. We have needed a book that addresses what it means to be single in the kingdom of God. Now we have it. This book was written by men and women who are part of the New York church ministry staff. Some writers are full time in the ministry and others work as administrators or children's ministry leaders. The topics discussed are as varied as the single lifestyle itself. Some of the topics covered are discipleship, finances, purity, dating, evangelism, spiritual living and relationships. Some of the chapters will overlap in themes, but we often need to be reminded of things more than once before we make lasting changes.

This book was written to encourage and build up singles in the kingdom. Read it with a Bible at your side and a pen in your hand. Underline it and mark it up. Make notes of the changes that you want to make, and pray about those changes. Share your goals with others and ask them to pray for you. Use the book in classes. Ask your ministry leaders to teach from the chapters in the book. Have a singles' workshop built around it. This is a book that deserves to be read and re-read. It was written by spiritually minded brothers and sisters, many of whom have lived as singles in the kingdom for years.

A special thanks is given to Steve and Lisa Johnson for their vision for singles across the kingdom over the years. Also, thanks to Tom and Sheila Jones, Kim Hanson and the staff at DPI for their help with the book. Thanks to my wife and kids because I don't thank them enough. And thanks to all the singles across the kingdom of God who continue to serve God and his kingdom with a "single-minded" focus. It is my prayer that this book will richly bless your lives.

G. STEVE KINNARD
NEW YORK CITY, USA

1

Undivided
Devotion to the Lord

DANIEL J. CONNER JR.

I would like you to be free from concern. An unmarried man is concerned about the Lord's affairs—how he can please the Lord. But a married man is concerned about the affairs of this world—how he can please his wife—and his interests are divided. An unmarried woman or virgin is concerned about the Lord's affairs: Her aim is to be devoted to the Lord in both body and Spirit. But a married woman is concerned about the affairs of this world—how she can please her husband. I am saying this for your own good, not to restrict you, but that you may live in a right way in undivided devotion to the Lord.

1 CORINTHIANS 7:32-35

Singles often see being unmarried as a curse or as a cross that they must bear until they are married. Singles, especially young singles, often feel like second-class citizens in the kingdom of God. However, Paul did not agree with this view. He believed that being single is a gift for which we ought to be grateful as long as we have it, because it is during this time of a person's life that he or she can focus solely on the Lord's affairs. Indeed, Paul seemed to think that it was only natural that someone who wanted to live "in a right way" would, without the added concern of a spouse, live "in undivided devotion to the Lord."

How do we live in undivided devotion to the Lord? The answer is simple: We must live in *undivided devotion to the Lord*. In other words, we must first be devoted. Next, the one to whom we are devoted must actually be our Lord. Third, that devotion must be undivided.

Consider the example of Mary Magdalene. In John 20:1-2 we read the following account of Mary at the empty tomb:

> Early on the first day of the week, while it was still dark, Mary Magdalene went to the tomb and saw that the stone had been removed from the entrance. So she came running to Simon Peter and the other disciple, the one whom Jesus loved, and said, "They have taken the Lord out of the tomb, and we don't know where they have put him!"

The disciples respond by running to the tomb and they also find it empty. However, "They still did not understand from Scripture that Jesus had to rise from the dead" (John 20:9). The story continues:

> Then the disciples went back to their homes, but Mary stood outside the tomb crying. As she wept, she bent over to look into the tomb and saw two angels in white, seated where Jesus' body had been, one at the head and the other at the foot.
>
> They asked her, "Woman, why are you crying?"
>
> "They have taken my Lord away," she said, "and I don't know where they have put him." At this she turned around and saw Jesus standing there, but she did not realize that it was Jesus. "Woman," he said, "why are you crying? Who

is it you are looking for?" Thinking he was the gardener, she said, "Sir, if you have carried him away, tell me where you have put him, and I will get him."

Jesus said to her, "Mary."

She turned toward him and cried out in Aramaic, "Rabboni!" (which means Teacher).

Jesus said, "Do not hold on to me, for I have not yet returned to the Father. Go instead to my brothers and tell them, 'I am returning to my Father and your Father, to my God and your God.'"

Mary Magdalene went to the disciples with the news: "I have seen the Lord!" And she told them that he had said these things to her.

In this single woman's life we find the model for what every disciple who is single must be.

Singularly Devoted

First, in order to live in undivided devotion to the Lord, we need to *be devoted*. Devotion requires an object; we must be devoted *to* something. In order to be devoted to the Lord, then, we must live our day-to-day lives for the Lord and not for ourselves.

Mary was devoted to Jesus and lived daily for him. While others often asked Jesus for miracles or signs, or argued about who was greatest, we are told of the women, including "Mary (called Magdalene)," who were with Jesus and his disciples and "were helping to support them out of their own means" (Luke 8:2-3). Again, we are told that when Jesus breathed his last, "many women were there, watching from a distance. They had followed Jesus from Galilee to care for his needs. Among them were Mary

Magdalene, Mary the mother of James and Joses..." (Matthew 27:55-56). Finally, when Jesus is laid in the tomb, Mary reacts by going home to prepare spices and perfumes for the body (Luke 23:56). Even after his death, she thinks only of serving him.

What was her secret? How could she have such a devotion to the Lord despite what would seem to be very painful times in her own life? How could she continue to think of him so selflessly when he seemed to have let her down?

The answer is simple, yet we often fail to put it into practice in our own lives. She served him because of who he was and what he had done. He had healed her and she was grateful. In the same way, we need to serve Jesus Christ because of who he is and what he has done for us, not for what he *will* do. Jesus Christ died on a cross for every single one of us. That should be enough. Gratitude needs to motivate us to be devoted to him.

There are many possible fringe benefits of being in the kingdom. We adopt a better and safer lifestyle. Our relationships improve. No longer do we have to put up with dishonesty, mistrust and gossip, nor must we put up with someone's moods just because "that is the way he is." We live by a standard that we can also call others to follow. Our lives have a new purpose—or, a purpose, period. Finally, we get to go to heaven for eternity when we die.

All of these can be motivations for being devoted to Jesus, but the primary motivation for us to follow Christ must be that he died for us on a cross. The love God has for us needs to be what inspires us to love him back. The fringe benefits, save going to heaven, are not guaranteed. Paul was imprisoned. His relationships were, no doubt, harder to maintain. Stephen was martyred. His life was not "better" from a worldly point of view. The same could be said of many other disciples. What kept them going was that they were not thinking about themselves, but about God.

Too often we struggle with living the lives of disciples of Jesus Christ only because we are in it for ourselves and not for Jesus Christ. When that happens, our feelings become the deciding factor in what we do. Yet in 2 Corinthians 5:14, we are told that the love of Christ compels us.

Most of us do not wake up every morning, jump out of bed, and shout, "I feel like serving God today!" There are times we do not feel like waking up, period, let alone in such an exuberant manner. But does that give us an excuse not to serve God? Absolutely not. Why? Because of the fact that no matter how we feel, Jesus died.

I remember hearing a preacher ask a group of people how they were feeling. Everyone responded with the usual hoots and hollers signifying that they felt wonderful. "Great," he replied, "but it doesn't matter. In the Bible, you are not told to feel, only to follow." His point was simple: not that we should pretend that we do not feel and become a group of robots, but that we cannot allow our feelings to dictate whether or not we follow Christ.

In order to be devoted to Christ, we must follow him and not ourselves and our feelings. To follow him we must be focused on him. Too often we watch ourselves trying to follow Christ, and do not look at Christ, whom we are supposed to be following. As a result, we get discouraged and selfish, and we turn the Bible into a self-help course which we must successfully complete.

I am reminded of a little girl I encountered while working as a teacher's aide in a day care center in Brooklyn as I completed my graduate work at NYU. She approached me one day and said, as she stared blankly into space, "Mr. Conner."

"Yes, Sofia?" I asked.

Without blinking or moving her head, she replied, "I'm daydreaming."

This is cute when a little girl says it. But some of us do the same, spiritually. Once Sofia realized she was daydreaming and started to think about herself doing so, her daydreaming stopped. The fact, then, that she was calling me to watch her daydream proved that she was no longer doing it.

Similarly, as disciples, if we take our eyes off Jesus and start to focus on ourselves following Jesus, we stop following Jesus. We cannot follow what we are not watching. When following Jesus stops being about Jesus and starts being about us, it merely becomes another task for us to accomplish, another achievement to add to our autobiography, another way to be a better person, and it ceases to be what it started as—a relationship with God.

When I talk to people who feel like giving up or who do not want to follow Jesus anymore, it is almost always because they have taken their eyes off Jesus and have been thinking only of themselves. They are looking at their sins or the times they have blown it or maybe their disappointments. They decide to quit because they think they will never measure up, or life will never be what they want it to be. That kind of thinking is selfish.

If we focus on God as we ought, our sin and our failures will cause us to realize that we have hurt him, which in turn will lead to even stronger convictions about repentance so that we will not hurt him again. It is only when we are focused on God like this, when we are truly devoted to him, that we can live the kind of life about which Paul writes.

Is Jesus Really Lord?

Second, in order to live in undivided devotion to the Lord, we must live in devotion *to the Lord*. In other words Jesus must be our Lord and master. He must call the shots in our lives.

Mary Magdalene again provides a striking example. Mary had gone through a great deal with Jesus. She had helped provide for his needs during his ministry. She was at the foot of the cross and even "saw the tomb and how his body was laid in it" (Luke 23:55). In Matthew 27:61, we find Mary "sitting there opposite the tomb." Finally, after discovering the empty tomb in John 20:2 she is distressed because "they have taken the Lord out of the tomb, and we don't know where they have put him!"

In other words, Mary Magdalene followed Jesus from Galilee to the empty tomb. She saw him mocked by the Pharisees and religious leaders. She watched as many of his followers left him. She saw one of his best friends betray him and the others desert him. She was with him as he was mocked, spit upon, flogged, beaten with a stick, punched repeatedly in the face and as a crown of thorns was driven into his skull. She watched as he staggered and fell under the weight of the cross, the same cross to which she saw his hands and feet nailed with metal spikes. She saw him slide up and down, gasping for air as he slowly suffocated...while the crowd laughed in his face. She heard him breathe his last and die. She stared as his lifeless body was placed in the tomb. She saw his followers hide in fear and even give up hope. Finally, she had to tell his disciples that his body had been taken from the tomb—she was appalled that the same Jesus who claimed to be the Messiah, the Son of God, had become so insignificant that someone could steal his corpse and hide it! Despite everything, Jesus never stopped being Mary's Lord. What stops him from being ours?

Lack of Faith

For some of us it is our belief that we are too weak to live the life of a disciple—to live according to the standard to which Jesus calls us. However, Paul, inspired by the Spirit, claims that we are able to resist any temptation to sin (1 Corinthians 10:13). To say we are too weak is to say that the Bible is untrue. Claiming to be too weak, or seeing ourselves as the exception, is an excuse to be selfish and to deny Jesus Christ.

Religious Past

For others of us, our religious past can keep Jesus from being our Lord. I came from a very religious background. I had been part of a youth group in the United Methodist Church in town since junior high school, a counselor at a Christian camp during high school, and went to a college where I attended chapel three times a week. I took various courses in theology, including church history, philosophy of theism and medieval philosophy. During that time, I went on two mission trips to Jamaica and one to Mexico, worked as a youth pastor in a Methodist church, preached to hundreds of teenagers at various youth rallies and retreats in a number of states, worked for the Salvation Army during Christmas vacations, took part in an inner-city ministry program in Brooklyn and toured the East Coast during spring break for three years as part of a troupe that performed plays with a moral or religious message. When I moved into Manhattan during my second year of graduate studies at New York University, I was looking for a church that was serious about God. I found one that was more serious than I was.

As I studied the Bible, I realized that in spite of my "spiritual resume" I was not living the life to which Jesus called his followers. Though I was religious, I continued to accept lust, impure relationships, deceit, gossip and pride as a regular part of life. I was neither living according to the standard of Jesus Christ, nor teaching his message.

I had a difficult decision to make. I realized that I needed to repent and begin to live the way the Bible said I should. I knew that to do so would mean that I would have to say that, despite all the things I had learned, I had not been doing what Jesus had called me to do. The temptation was to walk away—to choose my past over the Bible. After battling with the decision, I realized that I could not let my past, during which I had done things out of a real desire to follow God, keep me from actually following him. I had to let go of the past in order to follow Jesus Christ.

I remember hearing a story a few years ago about a woman in New York City who tried to board a subway just as the doors were closing. She stuck her purse between the closing doors in an attempt to make the conductor open them so that she could squeeze in. The conductor did not see her, and the train began to move. The woman attempted to free her purse from the door of the train, but it would not budge. She began to run alongside the moving train, clutching her purse. The people within shouted frantically, "Let go!" She did not listen. As the train gained speed, she was pulled off balance and onto the tracks where she was crushed.

The only thing the woman needed to do in order to live was to let go of the purse she thought was so valuable. In the same way, many of us hold on to our pasts even though they are pulling us to our destruction. We need to make Jesus Lord and let go of anything that keeps us from truly following him.

Relationships

Others of us allow our relationships to keep us from making Jesus Lord. We feel lonely, so we are willing to compromise our standard in order to feel loved. We give in to the pressure of the crowd to be like them and to stop being "religious fanatics." We get tired of feeling at odds with our families and friends who believe differently than we do. We sacrifice Jesus in order to love our friends.

Choosing to be a true disciple meant saying that I had been wrong. Furthermore, it would separate me from my friends who believed what I formerly believed. I remember thinking that I could not do it because I loved my friends too much. But then I realized that if I truly loved my friends, I would have to follow the truth. Otherwise, how would they ever know the truth? To choose against the truth in order to keep their approval for me was to not love them. Such a decision would mean sacrificing their eternity and loving no one other than myself.

Independence

Still others allow a deluded sense of freedom to get in the way. We refuse to make Jesus Lord because we know that we must submit to him and to others and live as part of his body (1 Corinthians 12; Philippians 2). We are part of a society that teaches us to do our own thing, not to listen to anyone, to just be. However, no one is really totally independent. We are constantly bombarded by messages from TV, radio, magazines, billboards and other mediums telling us how to live, what to wear, what ought to be important.

It is funny that people do not recognize the effects of these influences on them. I remember talking to a guy who rejected my invitation to a Bible discussion because he believed that he ought to make his own decisions, uninfluenced by others. Meanwhile, he looked exactly like the Gap ad on the bus station down the street. Teenagers today want to be rebellious but will not wear sneakers unless all of their peers approve of them. I am not saying that we should not be in style with our dress or not be relatable to people (see Chapter 7), but we should not walk around with the deluded notion that we can possibly live without being influenced by someone. In the words of Bob Dylan, "You gotta serve somebody...." To follow Jesus is simply to stop listening to the world and to let Jesus call the shots.

Finally, many of us let our selfishness stop Jesus from being our Lord. Again, the world teaches us to do what we want, that what we desire is best. It claims that anything that gets in the way of our getting what we want is bad. This reasoning, however, is ridiculous. For what we want is not always what we need. Anyone who has ever worked with children can testify to the truth of this. Almost every child desires something daily that is not only not what he or she needs, but is something that would be detrimental to the child. To allow children to do whatever they want to do—to run in the street, to play with scissors, to punch their classmates—would be cruel. Most people, and certainly most state laws in this country, agree with this.

There are other things that prevent Jesus from being our Lord that are less intentional, that even those who have decided to follow him allow to creep in and get in the way. Consider just a few:

Fear

We become afraid of what others will think of us if we stand out from the crowd. We do not talk to people and give them a chance to know God because we are afraid of being rejected. We stop serving Jesus so as not to offend anyone.

Unresolved Conflict

We get our feelings hurt and stop letting Jesus call the shots. We refuse to forgive, to love, to be humble when "wronged" and to work out our problems the way Jesus tells us to in Matthew 18. As a result, we walk around with bitterness and anger in our hearts, refusing to listen to God. We insist on our "right" to be respected while endangering ourselves with the fires of hell (Matthew 5).

Laziness

As single Christians, we have more time to help people make it to heaven than anyone else. The problem is that this fact is not reflected in enough of our schedules. Many of us are often discouraged because we have not been fruitful. We start to feel like God has abandoned us. In the meantime, though, we do not spend time reaching out to others. God has not left us; we are simply not walking with him. It is quite difficult to make disciples of all nations if we do not spend time with the people living in those nations! In order to do that we must give our time to God. We will be neither fruitful nor happy until we let Jesus be the Lord of our time.

Whatever our excuses, one look at Mary Magdalene is enough to shut our mouths. She lived in undivided devotion to the Lord by making Jesus Lord despite all kinds of circumstances.

To Will One Thing

Finally, in order to live in undivided devotion to the Lord, we need to have a devotion to the Lord that is *undivided*. Once again, we find an example in Mary Magdalene. When the other disciples find that Jesus is in fact missing, John tells us that they "went back to their homes" (John 20:10). The disciples go home but Mary stays. Why?

The Scriptures tell us that Peter later resumed his fishing, and the other disciples may have contemplated picking up their lives where they left off when Jesus called them. But this was not so easy for Mary. In Mark 16:9 we read,

When Jesus rose early on the first day of the week, he appeared first to Mary Magdalene, out of whom he had driven seven demons.

The other disciples could return to their homes and perhaps their old lives. Mary could not. She had nowhere to go. She would not return to demon possession. When Jesus saved her, he changed her life completely and forever. She stood outside the tomb crying because if Jesus was not Lord, life as she knew it was over. She had placed everything on Jesus' lordship. She had no chips left.

Can we say the same? How much of our lives have we invested in Jesus? How different would our lives really be if we stopped following Jesus tomorrow? For too many of us, the only change would be in our schedule: We'd sleep later on Sunday and have a midweek night free. If this is true of you, you need to repent! Jesus called us to total commitment, and it must show in how we live our lives.

Mary belonged totally to Jesus. He was all she had. "As she wept," we read (John 20:11) "she bent over to look into the tomb." Why? She could not give up. There was no turning back. She had made the decision to follow Jesus and she had no "Plan B."

Sometimes people try to follow God while leaving themselves a way out "just in case." They do not totally commit but try instead to have a back door through which to sneak out if the going gets tough. It is impossible to follow God that way. Jesus himself said, "Any of you who does not give up everything he has cannot be my disciple" (Luke 14:33). Jesus wants all or nothing.

When we refuse to give all, when we try to follow Jesus without having totally let go of the world, we quickly become burdened. Following Jesus becomes a miserable task because we never get what we want. We are unhappy living the life of a disciple because it conflicts with our worldly desires. Yet we are unhappy fulfilling the latter because we feel guilty when we do. So we equate discipleship with that misery and walk away. The problem is that the misery is not caused by discipleship but by halfhearted discipleship, straddling the fence between Christ and the world—which is really not discipleship at all.

When I was a child, my mother, frustrated by the recurring slam of the screen door as I entered and exited the house, would finally yell, "In or out!" She wanted me to make a decision and stop trying to be both places at once. God challenges us with the same ultimatum. We must walk in the light or in the dark. Trying to walk in between, in God's eyes, is walking in the dark.

Mary chose to follow Jesus completely, to walk in the light, to will one thing. The reason? Jesus had saved her from demon possession. She had no interest in going back to that terrible way of life, a life of powerlessness and misery. When we start looking back to our lives before Christ with regret for what we lost, we are forgetting the demons that controlled our lives: alcohol, drugs, lust, immorality, empty relationships, insecurity, hopelessness and powerless religion. Mary was grateful to be free of that life and knew that Jesus had saved her from it. He was all she needed and, therefore, all she wanted. Thinking he was the gardener, she said, "Tell me where you have put him, and I will get him" (John 20:15).

Is he enough for us? God sent Jesus to die on a cross so that we could have a relationship with him and be saved from sin, hell and meaningless lives. What more do we want? When we are not satisfied with Jesus, we either do not understand what he did, or we have forgotten. Only when we keep him and what he has done for us at the forefront of our hearts and minds, will we be able to live in undivided devotion.

The result of Mary's living this way was that she was among the first to see the risen Lord face to face. In order for us to see him one day as well, we must follow her example. If we live in undivided devotion to the Lord, then, and only then, can we say one day with Mary, "I have seen the Lord!" (John 20:18).

Focus Thought

I am not my own;
I was bought at a very high price.

2

Dreams

CINNAMON CONNER

I am writing this article less than a week before the fulfillment of a childhood dream. By the time you read this, I will be married to not only my best friend but the man of my dreams! At this point in my life, I feel especially qualified to write about dreams.

Of course, the dreams I am referring to are not the ones you have while you are sleeping. I am referring to the ones you must be fully awake to experience. In fact, if they are not specific, well thought-out, obvious to those who are close to you and something you are actively striving toward, they aren't dreams. I will take it a step further. We not only need dreams, we need spiritual dreams—those that are consistent with God's heart and nature and revolving around advancing his kingdom and his plans in *his* way.

Psalm 37:4 gives us the spiritual foundation for all of our dreams: "Delight yourself in the LORD and he will give you the desires of your heart." There it is! That is how we can know for sure if our desires are godly. Delighting in the Lord is the key.

Biblical Dreamers

In the Bible, examples of single men and women with godly dreams and ambitions abound. Not piddly itsy-bitsy dreams, either. I'm talking big, impossible, change-the-world, put-that-guy-on-*60-Minutes* kinds of dreams.

Just look at David. He was ducking Saul's spears and hiding out in caves, yet he had a dream to lead God's people and refused to compromise his righteousness and integrity to save his own hide. He realized that saving hides is God's business. David went on to become a king after God's own heart (1 Samuel 13:14) and designed the blueprint for a palatial home for the Great I AM to live in.

How about Ruth? She put the needs of her mother-in-law first, sacrificed what seemed to be her only chance of getting married again and trekked off to a distant foreign land. What did it get her? Oh, just a majorly spiritual husband and a place in the lineage of the Son of God.

One of my favorite men who dreamed is Joseph. He was going to be the "Big Sheaf," and all his older brothers were going to bow down to him. Not only his family, but the whole solar system would be doing big dippers at his feet (Genesis 37:5-9). Joseph had much to learn about bragging. He should have reserved his boasting for the Lord, and then maybe he would not have started out in such a big pit. Thank God he learned the lesson and was given future opportunities for giving glory to God (Genesis 40:8-41:16).

Despite Joseph's initial blabbering blunder, he gives us an excellent example of how to get great dreams for God. Now we may not currently have a dream about what God's plan is for our lives, but we certainly have a direct link to God through prayer, which is the place to start. If you do not have a dream from God, begin by asking God to reveal his will for your life. Pray about the things you would like to do. Be creative. Pray for the impossible, the improbable and the seemingly unlikely. Remember who you are *with* God: "What is impossible with men is possible with God" (Luke 18:27).

Share your dreams and ideas with your friends. If you are afraid to talk about your plans, then they are really more wishful thinking than dreams. (Stay tuned for some tips on how to defeat those pesky dream-stealing lies Satan and our own minds can throw at us.)

In short, Joseph was confident in his dream. We all need to be eager for input and direction about our dreams from those spiritually closest to us. But in the end it is you, God and your conviction. Live on the edge—out there in "I know I can't do this but God can" land. To quote a saying coined by one of our dynamic young ministers, "Don't just be. It's like living in a parenthesis—kinda there and kinda not there."

God loves uniqueness. After all, he created flamingos and flying squirrels! He will certainly put no less thought into using your life in a unique and powerful way in his kingdom. "According to your faith it will be done to you" (Matthew 9:29).

Joseph definitely had to live through a few nightmares along the way, and so will we. He had to really persevere to fulfill the dream God had for his life. It was not an easy road. He had many a setback to overcome. He was betrayed and deserted by his own flesh and blood, exposed to sexual temptation and punished for *not* giving in; he withstood a long incarceration and was forgotten by those he had helped. Talk about a prime breeding ground for bitterness and a big fat bad attitude!

Maybe you are going through some challenges in your dreams right now. If not, believe me—you will. That character sin you thought you had dealt with comes back. You are unjustly accused at your job and might get fired. You are battling some health problems and feel imprisoned by your own body. You are in the "always the bridesmaid and never the bride" pit. It seems as if no one ever notices how much you serve. You fall into the old "I want a pat on the back" syndrome. These are times when the spiritual rubber hits the road. The temptation to compromise, lie, get resentful or just give up altogether pounds on the door of your heart. How will you answer? Joseph faced these same temptations. His positive response, however, transformed each setback into a step forward for God. Don't think his is just a nice story. It can also be your story. Do you know what to call "temptations met with the truth"? Training ground!

Fighting to Keep Your Dreams

I marvel at how Joseph was able to stay righteous with only his conscience and his love for God to keep him on the straight and narrow. As disciples, we have the Spirit of God to guide us, the Bible to equip and direct us in every situation, and brothers and sisters all around us to help us along the way. But we have got to train ourselves. Don't grow weary or lazy in using the truth. Its power will defeat Satan and our sinful thinking *every* time. Have the sword of the Spirit ready for battle (Ephesians 6:17) and you can overcome lies like these:

"I believe God can do the impossible. I'm just not sure if he will for me."

> Commit to the LORD whatever you do,
>   and your plans will succeed (Proverbs 16:3).

"I've got my head on straight, and I know what's best for my life. I don't need to get advice on what I want to do."

> Plans fail for lack of counsel,
>   but with many advisers they succeed (Proverbs 15:22).

"I'm doing everything I can to be a great disciple, and I have great dreams for God, but it seems like nothing is happening."

> The Lord works out everything for his own ends—
>   even the wicked for a day of disaster (Proverbs 16:4).

"I hate discipline!"

> He who ignores discipline despises himself,
>   but whoever heeds correction gains understanding
> (Proverbs 15:32).

All of these Scriptures come from *one page* of my Bible. And I know everyone who reads this book has probably wrestled with these lies and doubts at some time or another. These dreambusters, and many others, are all defeatable with God. Rely on him and his strength as Joseph did, and experience the deepening of your faith which only refinement by fire can provide (1 Peter 1:7).

The greatest dreamer of them all is certainly Jesus. He shows us even more clearly that Satan flees when confronted by the words of God (Luke 4:1-13).

The kingdom and its advancement to all people in every nation is the fulfillment of God's dream for "all men to be saved and to come to a knowledge of the truth" (1 Timothy 2:4). This dream must be the dearest one to the heart of every disciple of Jesus because it is his dream. Pray specifically, ask for lots of input, share your ambitions and desires for God, never settle and never quit, so that when the smoke clears God can say to you, "Well done, good and faithful servant!" (Matthew 25:21).

FOCUS THOUGHT

I must dream big *today*,
but remember that God is even bigger
than my dreams.

3

Godliness
Is for Singles Too

MICHAEL A. SAGE AND MARSHA HYMAN

> But you, man of God, flee from all this, and pursue righteousness, godliness, faith, love, endurance and gentleness.
>
> *1 TIMOTHY 6:11*

When I (Mike) was making my decision to be a disciple of Jesus Christ, a minister from the church was talking to me about my dating life. He asked me what I thought about dating as a Christian. I told him that I was not going to go on dates anymore. He was very confused, but I explained to him that I thought I was never allowed to go on any dates because I had been immoral before becoming a Christian. I was fully convinced in my mind that I would not be allowed to date ever again in my life because of the way I had been in the past. In my heart, I felt that I did not deserve to date any women. I was willing to be single my entire life in order to become a disciple. To my relief, however, the minister laughed and told me that dating is permissible and encouraged, but not in the way I used to date in the world.

As a Christian, it is an honor and privilege to go on dates, to eventually have a girlfriend and then a wife. Do you see dating as an honor and privilege, or do you look at it as something you are entitled to and deserve? The most important issue in my life back then was being righteous in God's eyes. I was not concerned about having a girlfriend, job or apartment; I just wanted to be like Jesus.

As Christians, our goal is to become more and more like Jesus Christ. As Paul states in Philippians 3:10, "I want to know Christ." Paul's life was consumed with knowing Jesus. He looked forward to being with Christ in heaven after the resurrection. Within a prison cell, Paul was happy with his life because his goal was Christ. This is the essence of godliness. Godliness is "God-like-ness." As we strive to be like Jesus, we are striving to be godly.

Being a single Christian presents some special challenges to our godliness. We may always be thinking in the back of our heads, "Who is that special brother or sister who will sweep me off my feet and marry me?" We can focus totally on this thought, but how does it help us to become more like God? Jesus said in John 14:6, "I am the way, the truth, and the life." He didn't say that a spouse is the way! We will never be satisfied as single Christians unless we take on the attitudes of the heart that God commands in the Scriptures.

Bible Study and Prayer

In our quest for godliness, we must be aware of the fact that prayer and Bible study are essential ingredients. At times, this simple concept is not fully implemented by many Christians. Our relationship with God and our desire to become more Christlike take discipline and investment, much more than in our relationships with each other. Once our relationship with God is deep and exclusive of distraction, we naturally will have deep, spiritual and pure relationships with each other. Paul writes in 1 Timothy 4:8,

> For physical training is of some value, but godliness has value for all things, holding promise for both the present life and the life to come.

Paul was not discounting bodily training, because he believed it was good. However, he believed it was much more important to have spiritual training, which can only come through incredible Bible study and prayer. Some Christians are disciplined enough to work out for hours or train for a particular sport, yet can't spend an hour in prayer and Bible study. There are even some Christians who can spend hours on the phone with a brother or sister and yet dedicate only minutes to God.

Bible study and prayer are not natural instincts for someone who has lived twenty or thirty years without them. So it may sometimes be difficult to be consistent in our Bible study and prayer. Paul makes it clear that it will take training. What it comes down to is that if we want something badly enough, we *will* work hard for it.

There have been times in my spiritual walk (Mike) when a couple of days would go by and I had not read my Bible or had great conversations with God. My week really reflected that; I was running on my own strength and talent. I remember being emotional, faithless and easily manipulated by Satan. Jesus alerted his disciples to always watch and pray so that they would not fall into temptation (Matthew 26:41). It is too easy for Christians to be "busy" with daily circumstances that can distract them from spending quality time with God.

Prayer—Just Do It!

Throughout the Bible, we see incredible events that happened as a direct result of prayer. Hannah, who was barren, prayed for a child, and God granted her desire because of her faith and her wholeheartedness (1 Samuel 1:27-28). Elijah diligently prayed that it would not rain for three and a half years, and God answered his prayer (James 5:17). Elijah did not doubt that God was going to prove himself faithful. Furthermore, when Daniel was threatened with being thrown into the lion's den, his immediate response was to get down on his knees and pray to God with thanksgiving and without worry (Daniel 6:10-11). As a result, God answered his prayer and delivered him from the mouths of the lions.

We are crazy to think that God will hear us if we do not pray. I (Marsha) remember that after graduating from college I was making a tough decision whether to move from Virginia, where I had a job lined up for me, to New York City, where there was no job waiting for me. I had to decide where I was going to do my best spiritually. I prayed intensely because I did not really want to make that move. However, after much prayer, I decided to move to NYC and look for a job. Due to trusting God with my life and being confident of our relationship, he blessed me with the perfect job for $4,000 more a year than I was going to be paid in Virginia! Prayer sets our minds and helps us to be on our guard.

Prayer filled with faith is inspiring to the one praying. Our conversations with God need to be honest, faithful and intimate. Our prayer needs to be focused less on our needs and more on becoming and thinking like God. If a Christian feels a dullness in his or her prayer life, the thing *not* to do is to stop conversing with God, which can be so easy to do. On the contrary, we need to find ways in which we can rejuvenate our prayer life, like writing out our prayers, taking prayer walks, praying with a friend and spending more and different time with God. Remember that prayer pleases God. His eyes are always open and his ears are always attentive to the people who delight in revering his name (2 Chronicles 7:15).[1]

Bible Study—Gotta Have It!

Our Bible study goes hand in hand with prayer. If we desire to become more like God every day, we have to spend time with him in the Word every day. David in Psalm 119:20 said, "My soul is consumed with longing for your laws at all times." Is this how you feel, or are your times in the Bible short and uninspiring? The Bible is powerful because it challenges us to change and calls us higher in our faith. Do you spend more time reading the newspaper or watching television than you spend in your Bible?

I remember when I was going through a time when I did not know what to read in the Bible. I was just flipping through it and reading anything that the pages opened to. As a result I got dull in my faith. I decided that my Bible study had to change. I called a friend and asked for help and prayed for God to change my heart so that I was consumed with his words. If you are feeling dull in your Bible

---

[1] For a great study of prayer see *Teach Us to Pray* (Woburn, Mass.: Discipleship Publications International, 1995).

study, you can study out topics or characters in the Bible. You can go through the Gospels and study about Jesus—a study which can never get dull because our goal is to become more like him every day![2]

Five Ways to 'Get a Life' and Become More Godly

1. Pray earlier than normal (Mark 1:35).
2. Pray with passion (Hebrews 5:7).
3. Pray more (1 Thessalonians 5:17).
4. Know your Bible (2 Timothy 2:15).
5. Put your hope in God's word (Psalm 119:81).

Godliness is not impossible to attain if our attitude is like Paul's: his sole desire was to become more like Christ (Philippians 3:10). The only way to become like Christ is to have powerful prayers and Bible study. We cannot allow our desires for a mate, a career or material things to supersede our desire to be like Jesus. As single Christians, if we put Christ first in our lives, God will fulfill our every desire—above and beyond our expectations (Psalm 37:4-6).

FOCUS THOUGHT

God first in my heart today—absolutely.

---

[2] Discipleship Publications International has printed several volumes in the Practical Exposition Series. These can be a great help to you as you seek deeper knowledge of the Scriptures.

Let Go and Let God

KEISHA WILLIAMS AND AUGUSTIN RODRIGUEZ

The world and its desires pass away, but the man who does the will of God lives forever.

1 JOHN 2:17

Perhaps you have heard how to catch a monkey—those little creatures with both intelligence and speed. The ingenious hunter uses nuts for bait, placing them inside a narrow space in a rock or inside a small hole in a tree trunk. The monkey finds the nuts, and in his delight wiggles his hand into the hole and grabs them. His hand becomes a fist full of nuts which cannot exit through the small hole. Because of his greed, the monkey will not release the nuts and thus becomes a willing party to his own capture: The tree will not release his hand, and the monkey will not release his meal. He struggles to free himself. But even as the hunters close in, the monkey continues to hold on. He holds on to his life and he loses it.

Gain the World

"What good will it be for a man if he gains the whole world, yet forfeits his soul?" (Matthew 16:26).

Let's suppose you accomplished everything in life that you set out to do. You achieve the world's definition of success. You are educated, financially secure, on a great career track and have lots of "friends," a home, a car, relationships with the opposite sex, approval, acceptance and praise from men. But imagine after maybe twenty-five years or so you have to hand it over to someone who comes after you who has not worked for it, as Ecclesiastes 2:18 and 21 talk about.

That was me (Keisha). I had attained the dictionary definition of the word "success." I wanted it and went after it with all my heart. At seventeen there was no stopping me. I wanted to be an actress, a performer. I moved to New York City to win the world. After leaving the American Musical and Dramatic Academy, I dove head first into a world where, far from being short of work, I began to turn down jobs one after the other. By the age of twenty I had toured France, England, Germany and Belgium! I was making great money, and like Solomon, "I denied myself nothing my eyes desired" (Ecclesiastes 2:10).

Anything I wanted I could buy. I dated a New York Knicks basketball player, a Red Sox baseball player and rubbed elbows with the rich and famous. But I began to think, *Is this it? Is this all there is to life? So what happens when I have everything I want: the man, the career, the money—then what?* I knew there was still something missing, a void that none of these things seemed to fill. So in order not to think about that, I kept myself extremely busy. I was the party girl, the crowd pleaser, never alone, always where the action was. (It was exhausting!) "Having lost all sensitivity, [I had given myself] over to sensuality so as to indulge in every kind of impurity, with a continual lust for more" (Ephesians 4:19).

I became the woman I said I'd never be: grumpy, insecure, miserable, sad and lonely. I became hard and bitter. I had put up so many walls to protect myself but wanted so badly to be loved and accepted for who I really was. I thought to myself, *If people really knew me, would they like me?* After all, I had compromised my morals and basically sold my soul. Like the monkey, I kept holding on; nothing would stop me. I would not let go of the world. "But the [one] who lives for pleasure is dead even while she lives" (1 Timothy 5:6). That's what the world does. It destroys our self-esteem and confidence by setting up false standards that we can never measure up to: the perfect body, the perfect job, the perfect relationship. The world deceives us until we are willing to do anything—starve ourselves, lie, kill, covet—to gain success, approval and acceptance.

As Solomon says again and again in Ecclesiastes, "Meaningless! Meaningless!" What is all the striving for? Can you take it with you? In 100 years, who will remember what a great actress, doctor or lawyer you were? No one, because you will be dead and so will they! "The world and its desires pass away, but the man who does the will of God lives forever" (1 John 2:17). The truth of the matter is that in time, all dead bodies look alike. We cannot tell the rich from the poor, the single from the married, the plain from the beautiful. The only thing that sets them apart is whether or not they had a relationship with God. Really, all that matters is where they will be spending eternity: in heaven with God or facing hell with Satan.

Think of one of your most pleasurable sinful moments in the world and ask yourself if it was worth it. Was it all that fun, that rewarding, that promising? What did you gain? Was it worth what it did to Christ? Our Savior was humiliated, tortured and brutally murdered—that's the price he had to pay for our sinful desires. "What benefit did you reap at that time from the things you are now ashamed of? Those things result in death!" (Romans 6:21). Worldliness kills!

Love the World?

"Do not love the world or anything in the world. If anyone loves the world, the love of the Father is not in him. For everything in the world—the cravings of sinful man, the lust of his eyes and the boasting of what he has and does— comes not from the Father but from the world" (1 John 2:15-16).

Satan is the ruler of this dark world. He masquerades as an angel of light, deceiving, lying, sweet-talking, taunting and charming us. The world is Satan's playground! But don't be deceived. He remembers the "games" we used to play, what interested us most, stole our focus, got us going. And he will gladly pay any price to provide the toys that will distract us as disciples, whispering, "These things will make you happy."

The question is: Can you be bought? What does he have to whisper in your ear to get you to flirt with the world? What is in the world that you desire? We cannot have both the world and the kingdom. We cannot serve two masters, and we are slaves to whatever masters us (Matthew 6:24; 2 Peter 2:19). James, the brother of Jesus, wrote:

"You adulterous people, don't you know that friendship with the world is hatred toward God? Anyone who chooses to be a friend of the world becomes an enemy of God."

JAMES 4:4

When we are desiring anything in or of the world, we're not just being "worldly," we're hating God! Jesus understood all too well that by giving in to worldly cravings, temptations or desires, he would be choosing not only to please Satan but to worship him.

Several months ago a disciple pursuing his dreams to be an actor decided to go on tour. Knowing that it probably would not be the best situation because the closest church was hours away, he decided to go anyway. The first few months were pretty good. He had started leading a Bible discussion group and traveled every weekend to church. But he eventually stopped. He became lazy, complacent and a walking target for Satan. He began to compromise his biblical convictions, skipping church in order to play roles that might eventually land him the lead. He began drinking and partying and ultimately turned away from God and left his wife (who continues to be a faithful disciple). Like Demas who loved the world (2 Timothy 4:10), this brother craved fame and fortune and deserted God.

Satan can deceive us so easily into worldly thinking. He does this without us even realizing what is happening. Take a heart test. Do any of these thoughts ever cross your mind?

• Is it so wrong to want to spend a little extra money on me?
• So, does God expect me to sell everything and live in the street?

- If I were not a disciple, I could look like that too.
- Go on! Live a little! You deserve a break!

If you love the world, you will eventually leave God. Loving the world gains you

- 60-70 years, maybe? (Psalm 90:10)
- Death (Romans 6:23)
- Worry (Matthew 6:34)
- Despair (Ecclesiastes 2:20)
- Disappointment (Ecclesiastes 5:10)
- Greed (Romans 1:28-31)
- Temporary gains (2 Corinthians 4:18)
- An unfruitful/unproductive life (Matthew 13:22)
- A jealous/competitive heart (James 4:1-3)

Overcome the World

"...for everyone born of God overcomes the world. This is the victory that has overcome the world, even our faith. Who is it that overcomes the world? Only he who believes that Jesus is the Son of God" (1 John 5:4-5).

As disciples of Christ who have been sealed with God's Spirit, we have the power to overcome anything. The resurrection is proof that Jesus was able to overcome even death. If we believe and have faith in the resurrection, we too will fight to overcome the world (John 16:33).

Sometimes it is difficult for us to believe we can really change. We ask ourselves, *Can I really be a spiritual man or woman of God?* Because the same things have controlled us for so long, we doubt our ability to change. But God has no doubts that we can change. Take his word and listen humbly.

Be Transformed

The first thing to remember is: "Do not conform any longer to the pattern of this world, but be transformed by the renewing of your mind" (Romans 12:2a). According to Paul, the way to overcome the world is to be transformed, and this begins with renewing our minds. When we become disciples, we get a new life. But we still carry a lot of old baggage from the world: its ideas, opinions, thoughts. We have to reconstruct our old ways of thinking— unspiritual and worldly—and replace them with the word of God. As Jesus was being tormented by Satan in the desert, God's word was all he used to overcome the temptations. If it worked for Jesus, it will work for us!

Set Your Hearts

The second thing to remember is to "set your hearts on things above...not on earthly things" (Colossians 3:1-2). We need to look at life with an eternal perspective and remember that our goal is heaven and not the things of this world. We must store up for ourselves treasure in heaven, not riches on earth (Matthew 6:19-21). We need to yearn for the day when we will meet our Father in heaven and think about all the friends we will have helped to get there. We cannot center our lives around getting a raise at work or the relationship of our dreams that we hope will make us complete. We were given talents by God not to serve ourselves or the world, but to build up and forcefully advance God's kingdom (Matthew 25:14-17). Remember that you were crucified with him and you no longer live (Galatians 2:20). It is no longer about what you want, what you think, what you need, but about what is best for God's kingdom and what will save the most souls.

Let Go

The third thing to remember is: "Put to death, therefore, whatever belongs to your earthly nature" (Colossians 3:5). Let go of those things that have had a hold on you, all the things you are grasping so tightly. Get rid of any "back doors" described in Chapter One—those places you can always run back to if things do not turn out the way you have planned. Your back door might be that relationship in the world that you still daydream about when you are not getting attention in the kingdom. Maybe it is the cushy, comfortable life you thought you might have. Sometimes the hardest thing to let go of is ourselves—we just have to trust that God has the best plan for our lives and believe that his way and his timing are best.

"Fear not, my little flock. It makes your Father happy to give you the kingdom.

Sell your possessions, and give to those in need. Make purses/wallets for yourselves that will never wear out and be discarded—an unfailing treasure in heaven that no thief can touch and no moth can destroy. Where your treasure is you will also find your heart" (Luke 12:32-34).[1]

[1] Translation by G. Steve Kinnard

I (Augustin) became a disciple while pursuing an acting career. I have played the part of a teenage mutant superhero in a made-for-TV movie entitled *Generation X* and have also appeared in the movies *Strange Days* and *Falling Down*. I have had the opportunity to work with Richard Gere, Kim Basinger, Michael Douglas, Eartha Kit, Carl Weathers and Ralph Finnes.

When I think back on my career now, I see how much my relationship with God has helped me to change. I have turned down many acting opportunities because they were unrighteous and not pleasing to God. I do not want to be involved in any roles that are against God. I am no longer concerned with what my colleagues think. I am no longer consumed by how my manager or my friends see me. What do men know anyway? They only see the outer man, but God sees the heart.

God has blessed me with two jobs. As an actor I currently have a guest-starring role in a popular TV show and a starring role in a TV movie of the week, and then I also have the honor of serving full time in the ministry for the Daytime (performing arts) Sector of the New York City church. God has let me use the gifts he has given me and has blessed me beyond my dreams (Psalm 37:4). I look back over my past accomplishments and, like Paul, I consider them all rubbish compared to the surpassing greatness of knowing Christ (Philippians 3:7-8).

When you "let go and let God," others will take notice. Take Angela Jones, for example. Angela is a talented ballerina. She was offered the role of a lifetime, but she turned it down because she believed the costume she was required to wear was ungodly. Everybody in her dance company was shocked. Three years later, a friend of hers in the dance company became a disciple because of Angela's example. When you "let go and let God," you influence others (1 Peter 2:11-12).

Unlike the monkey who greedily grasped his treasure to his own demise, disciples release their dreams and allow God to reshape them. We surrender our dreams to God!

> "We no longer need preeminence, prosperity, position, promotions, plaudits, or popularity. We don't have to be right, first, tops, recognized, praised, regarded, or rewarded. We now live by presence, lean by faith, walk by patience, lift by prayer, and labor by power. Our faith is set, our gait is fast, our goal is heaven, our road is narrow, our way is rough, our companions few, our guide reliable, our mission clear. We cannot be bought, compromised, detoured, lured away, turned back, deluded, or delayed. We will not flinch in the face of sacrifice, hesitate in the presence of the adversary, negotiate at the table of the enemy, ponder at the pool of popularity or meander in the maze of mediocrity. We are part of the fellowship of the unashamed.
>
> We have the Holy Spirit's power. The dye is cast. We have stepped over the line. The decision has been made. We're disciples of his. We won't look back, let up, slow down, back away or be still—until he comes."
>
> Bob Moorhead

For the grace of God that brings salvation has appeared to all men. It teaches us to say 'No' to ungodliness and worldly passions, and to live self-controlled, upright and godly lives in this present age, while we wait for the blessed hope—the glorious appearing of our great God and Savior, Jesus Christ, who gave himself for us, to redeem us from all wickedness and to purify for himself a people that are his very own, eager to do what is good (Titus 2:11-14).

FOCUS THOUGHT

I will never lose by trusting God

Sexual Purity in a Calvin Klein World

T.S. GRANT AND ANNA LEATHERWOOD

> Don't let anyone look down on you because you are young, but set an example for the believers in speech, in life, in love, in faith and in purity.
>
> *1 TIMOTHY 4:12*

Sexual purity sounds like a very old-fashioned idea in our society. Maintaining it is no longer on the list of priorities for singles or for marrieds. Every imaginable form of impurity is now accepted. Everything from blue jeans to beer is sold with sexual images. What once was the television networks' "family hour" is now a time when one hears all kinds of lewd remarks and sexual innuendoes. The great majority of references to sexual activity concern people who are not married to each other. The story is not that different among religious people who are often only vaguely committed to purity if they are committed to it at all. Women and men who follow Jesus Christ follow a different standard altogether, and both women and men need to know that they can win the battle with lust and find incredible satisfaction by pursuing the purity God desires.

Conquering Lust: A Woman's Perspective

Karen was an attractive young woman determined to make her mark on the world. One night she and all of her girlfriends went out to a bar. She spent the evening in the smoke-filled bar, talking, dancing and drinking with her friends. Not too far away at a table in the corner a man had been watching her throughout the night.

As she was getting ready to go back to her apartment, someone approached her. He pointed at the man sitting in the dark corner and explained that he was a billionaire who wanted to speak with her. Intrigued, she asked, "What is this about?" But the man just told her to come with him. After she had asked her friends to wait for her, she followed him over to the table.

"Have a seat," he said, as he motioned for her to sit. "I have to tell you that you are an attractive young lady. I hope this doesn't embarrass you, but I've been completely enamored by you all night. Being a man of great wealth, I am used to getting whatever I want. I am prepared to grant you whatever payment you think is acceptable. I want to have sex with you, one time, no strings attached. Name your price."

"What kind of woman do you think I am? You think you can just make an offer like that and I'll state an amount and that's it?" Disgusted, she stormed away.

He merely smiled. *She will come around,* he thought to himself.

Time went by, and she thought of the proposition he had made. Every time she went into that bar, a nod in her direction let her know the offer was still good. Financial difficulties in her family, coupled with the desire to live a pampered life, were making his proposition more and more appealing.

Finally, one night she went over to his table at the bar and sat down. "I've been thinking it over, and I want to make some things clear. One time, right? And I can name the price?"

"Just as I told you before. The rules are still the same," he replied.

"Okay. I want one million dollars," she responded apprehensively.

"Great! We need to arrange a time and a place," he said. "I knew you would come around. Now, would you do it for a hundred dollars?"

Bewildered, she exclaimed, "What kind of woman do you think I am?!"

"Don't act so offended, my dear. We know what kind of woman you are—now we are just negotiating a price."

Are you for sale? If we are for sale, Satan will pay the price. We are God's now! If we can be bought at *any* price, we are prostitutes. Just as that man cared nothing for that young woman, Satan cares nothing for us! He is prowling around looking for a way to make us compromise our convictions (1 Peter 5:8). Our defense against him is to be alert and self-controlled. All women face an emotional and physical battle for purity at some point. We also need to battle the temptation of wanting men to lust after us, which many of us do not even recognize as being sinful. We need to know our weaknesses and how to turn them into our strengths. Everyone sins, but every person has different desires and different temptations. We have to be honest about the struggles we face to expose the way Satan tries to manipulate our minds and hearts. Let's look at four women and the desires they face. More than likely you will relate to each of them in some way. I know I do.

Sue of the Harlequin Romance

Sue's favorite movie is *Snow White*. "Someday My Prince Will Come" is her theme song. She does not see a handsome man and immediately imagine being in bed together. Most of her thoughts are day-dreamy, fluffy, knight-in-shining-armor-sweeping-her-off-her-feet thoughts. People are amazed by her innocent ways and gentle nature. Her Christian friends are impressed that she rarely confesses impure thoughts. However, she rarely has a conversation without including dating, marriage and romance in it. At church, she looks around for her future husband instead of future disciples. She carries her calendar to plan dates, not Bible studies.

"And we know that in all things God works for the good of those who love him" (Romans 8:28). As disciples we have the hope and faith that God will give us what we need. We have to want God's will—his way and his timing. The goal of our lives is to please God, not to be married. When our focus turns away from God and onto ourselves, we become foolish. Satan gains a foothold in our hearts. Solomon wisely wrote that someone "who chases fantasies lacks judgment" (Proverbs 12:11). Be open with your thoughts, dreams and insecurities with God and with the disciples around you. Prayer moves God's heart; it also moves our hearts. It is always more challenging to trust

God in matters of the heart, but he loves us and gives us exactly what we need.

Mary, Queen of Emotions

Mary is emotional. She struggles with believing that God has her best interest at heart. Jeremiah 29:11 has become harder and harder for her to believe. She often feels lonely. Younger, prettier, slimmer women are not friends and sisters but rivals and competitors. Jealousy and envy have begun to blind her. As a result, friendships with other women are difficult. She considers dating men in the world because no Christian men seem interested in her. Strange thoughts have taken over her mind like, *I don't want to have sex with someone; I just want someone to hold me.* She says to herself, "I just want someone to think I'm special." Mary's emotional insecurity makes her a prime target for unspiritual men and impurity.

The world has taught us that sex equals love. This can take quite a toll on us emotionally. When we are not close to people, we naturally begin to feel lonely. We have all experienced loneliness at some point, even as Christians. The danger in not being close to people is that we can begin to feel insecure. The feeling that we are not needed or that we are not loved can often lead us to look for the wrong kind of attention: sexual attention. Love, according to 1 Corinthians 13, is very different from what the world teaches us about it. As disciples, we have the opportunity to be emotionally bonded to our Creator and to his children. Loneliness is a tool of Satan to cause us to struggle with lust and even to be impure. Love is not sex. Love is a decision. We must decide to give our hearts to people. Then we can learn the real closeness that is possible in relationships.

Tonya with the Roaming Eyes

Tonya's biggest weakness is lust of the eyes. A gorgeous man or a lewd advertisement causes her thoughts to run rampant. She thinks about where she could go with that man and what he would be like in bed. She is aware of every "hot" guy in the room after being there for only two minutes. When there is an opportunity for her thoughts to go to impurity or lust, they do. When there is no "opportunity," she makes one.

Our minds are the battleground for so many of Satan's attacks. According to 1 Corinthians 2:16, we are supposed to have the mind of Christ. Do we? Training our minds takes every ounce of self-control we have. Paul teaches us in 2 Corinthians 10:5 that we must take captive our thoughts. This takes training. We have to learn to imprison evil thoughts as they are going through our minds and make them spiritual.

Suppose you are with a man who is very gentle. You are tempted to imagine him being gentle with you in a sexual way. Instead, think that because he is so gentle, he will be a great father. Then think about how God is such a great father to us. Then Satan will have lost that opportunity. In Matthew 4, Jesus is being tempted by the devil. How does he fight? His mind was filled with Scripture. Whatever we think about is what we become. Remember Paul's admonition in Philippians 4:8:

Finally, brothers, whatever is true, whatever is noble, whatever is right, whatever is pure, whatever is lovely, whatever is admirable—if anything is excellent or praiseworthy—think about such things. ·

It is dangerous when we start minimizing sin. We think, "I just want someone to think I am special." We want a longer hug, another kiss, and before we realize it, we are involved in impurity. Remember that temptation begins as desire (James 1:13-15). What do we long for? Learning to take hold of our feelings and desires is a sign of spiritual maturity. The Psalmist stated, "Whom have I in heaven but you? And earth has nothing I desire besides you" (Psalm 73:25). Call sin what it is.

Veronica, the Princess of Subtle Signals

All of Veronica's life her security and pleasure have come from being noticed. There was never a time that a pair of eyes glanced at her twice and she did not notice it. She knows how to walk with just the right amount of sway in the hip, how to speak with a slightly sensuous tone, how to dress on the edge. When men talk to her, they feel entranced. This is just how she likes it. Her Christian friends would not call her flirtatious because she is subtle. But some men notice her signals, and they are uncomfortable with them. She would do well to heed Luke 17:1-3:

Things that cause people to sin are bound to come, but woe to that person through whom they come.... So watch yourselves.

She becomes a hindrance to those around her because she concerns herself very little with protecting the purity of others.

All too often we are more concerned with how people see *us* rather than how people see God. The Apostle Peter spoke of the importance of example in 1 Peter 3:1-4:

> ...they may be won over...when they see the purity and reverence of your lives. Your beauty should not come from outward adornment, such as braided hair and the wearing of gold jewelry and fine clothes. Instead, it should be that of your inner self, the unfading beauty of a quiet and gentle spirit, which is of great worth in God's sight.

We need to have a conviction that when we want to be lusted after, we are causing others to sin. It is stupid for us to want to be desirable in a physical way to men:

> For everything in the world—the cravings of sinful man, the lust of his eyes and the boasting of what he has and does— comes not from the Father but from the world (1 John 2:16).

Our purpose is to lead others to God, not deeper into sin.

We have already won the battle. Jesus bought us with his blood (1 Peter 1:18-19). We are constantly purified, as long as we walk in the light (1 John 1:7). The fact that we have been rescued and are continuously cleansed should be our motivation to live self-controlled and pure lives. When we get truthful, we get help and get grateful. Then we can be victorious!

Conquering Lust : A Man's Perspective

Imagine this modern dramatization based on the first two chapters of the book of Job:

One day the angels came to present themselves before the Lord, and Satan also came with them. The Lord said to Satan, "Where have you come from?"

Satan answered, "From roaming through the earth and going back and forth in it."

Then the Lord said, "Have you considered my servant Joe? There is no one like him. He is blameless and pure."

"Sure," replied Satan, "he has so many disciples around him. You have put a hedge around him; that's why he is so pure. I bet if I get him alone, he won't be so 'awesome'!"

The Lord said to Satan, "Whether alone or with many, his love for me remains the same."

Meanwhile, in the spiritual realms, wagers were already being placed on his battle with temptation. A rookie demon said, "I bet he will sin."

Another demon said, "It's not if he'll sin, it's when. I say he won't even pray about it or ask his God for help."

The rookie demon responded, "Maybe you're right. He doesn't seem to ask for much help. Although, he does confess a lot afterwards..."

The older demon interrupted, "Okay. Put up or shut up. I bet he sins but not right away. In his mind he'll think he's fighting sin by being neutral—not fleeing sin but not physically sinning either. But his mind will still be working. I give him forty-eight hours, and he'll give in. Give me a couple of days with him. He's smarter than you think, but not as smart as he thinks. Forty-eight hours or no deal."

Can you see the reality of the spiritual battle for self-control, for victory over impurity? Ephesians 6:10-12 states:

> Finally, be strong in the Lord and in his mighty power. Put on the full armor of God so that you can take your stand against the devil's schemes. For our struggle is not against flesh and blood, but against the rulers, against the authorities, against the powers of this dark world and against the spiritual forces of evil in the heavenly realms.

Notice that our spiritual battle is against "the rulers, authorities and powers of this dark world." Satan absolutely does not hold back. If you struggle with lust and have a difficult time controlling yourself, then this chapter is for you. It will provide you with insight into purity that will help you battle temptation.

> And without faith it is impossible to please God, because anyone who comes to him must believe that he exists and that he rewards those who earnestly seek him (Hebrews 11:6).

Self-control is an issue of faith. We must *believe* we can win the battle over lust.

> So I say, live by the Spirit, and you will not gratify the desires of the sinful nature. For the sinful nature desires what is contrary to the Spirit, and the Spirit what is contrary to the sinful nature. They are in conflict with each other, so that you do not do what you want (Galatians 5:16-17).

The Spirit and the flesh are in conflict. I used to think that I was a pure-hearted disciple who forgot how to sin and what sin was. After many struggles with lust, I learned how much in error I was.

Galatians 5:16-17 teaches us that even though we have the Spirit of Christ in us, we have to make a decision to live by his Spirit. There is a conflict of interest between the Holy Spirit and the sinful nature. We must learn to rely on the Spirit. The Spirit, like Jesus, would never get us into a headlock and force us to obey. He will not hold us down and remove money from our pockets so we cannot buy pornography; nor will he remove scantily dressed women from the streets. The Holy Spirit is our counselor; we must all decide if we will listen and obey. We must believe that the Spirit is in us, that God exists in us, or else we will not survive the battle.

For some the struggle is greater than it is for others. The apostle Paul begged for God to remove an unnamed "thorn in his flesh," but God would not remove it:

> [God] said to me, "My grace is sufficient for you, for my power is made perfect in weakness." Therefore I will boast all the more gladly about my weaknesses, so that Christ's power may rest on me" (2 Corinthians 12:9).

With God's Spirit in us we are set to win. I have studied the Bible with hundreds of men, and I have never met someone more perverse in mind and action than I was before I became a disciple. I do not say this as a boast but as a confession. I was enslaved to impurity and sex. Since I have been a Christian, over four years, I have consistently had victories over impurity—to God be the glory! He has empowered me.

My mind is very creative. I used to be a comedian for the US Air Force. This creativity is a gift and tool from God that became a weapon for Satan. My struggle would always start with my imagination and lead me into sin. My own desires were the beginning point, and I was entirely responsible for the sin that resulted:

> When tempted, no one should say, "God is tempting me." For God cannot be tempted by evil, nor does he tempt anyone; but each one is tempted when, by his own evil desire, he is dragged away and enticed. Then, after desire has conceived, it gives birth to sin; and sin, when it is full-grown, gives birth to death (James 1:13-15).

As a disciple now I have to "take captive every thought to make it obedient to Christ" (2 Corinthians 10:5). This is a high standard, but it is the standard of discipleship. We must use this standard in every area of our lives: on the job, while dating, during leisure time and hobbies and in our choices of movies and entertainment options.

If we really believe that Jesus Christ is with us, which is true for anyone who has been baptized into him, we will exercise more self-control. Did not Jesus promise, "and surely I am with you always, to the very end of the age"? (Matthew 28:20b). Anyone who denies this is unspiritual, and most likely unwilling to change.

A good question to ask yourself is, "What if everything my eyes fixed on today was videotaped and played before the church on Sunday (without a narrative of explanation)?" What would it reveal? Buttocks, legs, breasts, lips, girl, girl, girl, belly button, *Hustler* magazine, lewd music videos?

Get the drift? Or would it show—a man (a potential brother), a woman (a potential sister), a child, the sky, a poor person, a passage of Scripture, an animal, etc.? Thinking this way helps my unspiritual rationalizations of, "Well, I am only looking," or "She looks familiar," or "I just admire women." Ask yourself if you admire the same things in your mother or sister that you do in other women. Would you want someone to "just admire" those things about your wife or your teenage daughter? (To be clear, it is not the flash of temptation that is sinful. No one can keep every sight that is not best out his eyes. It is what we do with it from that point forward: dismiss it or dwell on it. Developing that thought or dwelling on it is sin. For too many, the flash of temptation becomes the freeze frame of sin.) Also, ask yourself, "What if she knew I was thinking about her this way?" I asked a spiritual sister how she would feel knowing a brother was lusting after her. She replied, "I would not want to be around him at all. I would feel violated and uncomfortable." My sister's response helped me understand that my thoughts must be controlled by how others might feel and what is best for them.

Practical Suggestions:

- Don't watch television or videos late at night (or maybe even alone).
- Take military showers—five minutes or less.
- Be open with any and all struggles.
- Never be alone in an apartment with a woman.
- Research your movies before going to them. If there is a sex scene, reconsider going. Forget, "I will just close my

eyes or plug my ears during that part," all the while looking weird, singing church songs or talking to your friend. Satan knows that you know what is happening on the big screen. Remember that it is not always what you see or do not see, it is what you think about what you see or do not see. Do not be surprised if you go see an R-rated movie and there are some nude scenes. I have missed many movies, but I've also missed out on many struggles. The last two practical points seem obvious but the absence of them is the number one reason why people struggle and sin:

- Have great daily Bible studies. "How can a young man keep his way pure? By living according to your word" (Psalm 119:9). When I am constantly in God's word, the temptation to lust seems so much less.
- Pray continually. Luke 18:1-8—read it.

I received a call a couple of weeks ago from a brother who had been struggling with impurity for months. This message was different. Now he was sharing his victories over impurity. I was so encouraged. He used to sin and confess, sin and confess. It was sad because I began to see him grow lukewarm in his discipleship. His confessions were mechanical and seemed scripted. He would always show signs of worldly sorrow but never repentance. At times, he was dramatic in his confessions. He would even exclaim, "I hate this, I do not want to hurt God." After many failures, he is now victorious. You too can be victorious in this area of life. That is true not just because some other men have been, but it is true because God is faithful and he has promised that with every temptation he will provide a way so you can stand up under it. You can overcome!

Homosexual Struggles

This section is for brothers who were practicing a homosexual lifestyle and are now repentant disciples, but still struggle with the sin. The basis for overcoming this sin is the same as with heterosexual lust: Faith is the victory! Homosexuals that I have studied the Bible with have told me, "You have hope as a heterosexual single, but I have no hope." They add, "You will be married and have an outlet for your lust. That will not happen to me." I always answer them by saying, "I became a Christian with the hope of going to heaven, not of getting married. You have to ask yourself if heaven is enough for you. Is God enough for you?"

I have met men who have been in the kingdom for quite some time as singles who have not struggled with impurity. My first roommate was an evangelist and single for thirteen years before he married. All that time he stayed pure for God. With God's power, we can control our lust.

I know many men who had homosexual pasts, became Christians and are now married with children. I do not claim to understand everything they experience, but I know God understands. His promise to help us overcome is for every person regardless of his or her temptations.

While there are some things I do not understand, I do understand enslavement and sexual addiction. Often sexual struggles begin in the mind. We need a mind change that will help curtail lust. To notice that a man is attractive is not wrong. To allow yourself to be attracted to him is wrong. Personally, I can note that even a married woman is attractive. This can serve to encourage her. But when I entertain lustful thoughts and allow myself to be attracted to her, that's when Satan wins because it is not right to allow myself to be attracted to a married woman. Such thoughts lead to destruction. I must fight this unspiritual attraction.

If you want to overcome your struggles, do not allow yourself to be attracted to a man. If he is in the world, what could the attraction possibly be? If he is a brother, do not entertain the thoughts. You must "treat younger men as brothers" (1 Timothy 5:1).

Conclusion

We never have the right to blame our circumstances. None of us can think we are exceptions when it comes to the need for self-control and purity. Paul wrote,

> I have been crucified with Christ and I no longer live, but Christ lives in me. The life I live in the body, I live by faith in the Son of God, who loved me and gave himself for me (Galatians 2:20).

We must long for purity. Consider the apostle John's words in 1 John 3:2-3,

> Dear friends, now we are children of God, and what we will be has not yet been made known. But we know that when he appears, we shall be like him, for we shall see him as he is. Everyone who has this hope in him purifies himself, just as he is pure.

As a disciple, you have been set up to win. I only hope that you will allow God to work in your life to turn your weaknesses into strengths. It can be done; it has been done. If your desire is great enough, you can win. If Jesus were coming back tomorrow, would you sin? Live as if Jesus were coming tomorrow. Live as if Jesus were walking with you today—because in fact, he is!

No, in all these things we are more than conquerors through him who loved us. For I am convinced that neither death nor life, neither angels nor demons, neither the present nor the future, nor any powers, neither height nor depth, nor anything else in all creation, will be able to separate us from the love of God that is in Christ Jesus our Lord (Romans 8:37-39).

FOCUS THOUGHT

The pure in heart will see God,
and I *want* to see God!
(See Matthew 5:8.)

6

Contentment in Every *Single* Circumstance

JODI DOUGLAS

> Now to him who is able to do immeasurably more than all we ask or imagine, according to his power that is at work within us, to him be glory in the church and in Christ Jesus throughout all generations, for ever and ever! Amen.
>
> *EPHESIANS 3:20-21*

"I want more!"—a phrase that summarizes my attitude toward life for eighteen years before I became a disciple. I wanted to be the most, the best, the everything. As a result, I excelled at many things, but in my own heart there was a continual dissatisfaction. As a disciple, this same attitude emerged. I was driven to do something great for God and desperately wanted to please him. Along with these seemingly spiritual ambitions, however, came a lack of contentment. I would often compare myself to others, feeling insecure if I felt I did not "measure up" or feeling jealous if I thought God was blessing someone with something he did not bless me with. Because I was focused on what God had not yet given me rather than on the abundance that he had, I owned a discontented heart. My thinking was so limited! I believed that if God did not bless me today that he must have decided not to bless me at all. I did not have a spiritual perspective on the future, having forgotten that life in Christ is a marathon and not a sprint.

On the night before my twenty-second birthday I read a scripture that has since changed my life. Ephesians 3:20–21 revealed how limited my view of God was. The Bible said that my God would do "immeasurably more than all I could ask or imagine," and I had imagined some amazing things! This passage was telling me how unlimited God is in his ability to bless us. The more I understood how powerful and bountiful God is, the more grateful I became, and this gratitude began guarding my heart against all the negative thinking that produces a discontented heart.

Centuries ago the apostle Paul taught Timothy the value of contentment in the midst of struggles when contentment seemed to be an elusive quality (1 Timothy 6:6-10). Even Paul himself, who witnessed a vision of heaven, had to "learn the secret of being content" (Philippians 4:12). If these heroes of the church had to focus on contentment, then I believe it is time for us also to wrestle with our hearts and expose the areas where we need to grow in our own contentment.

Test Your Heart

Answer the following questions to see how content your heart really is.

1. When negative thoughts enter your mind, can you quickly remember God and throw them off, or are these thoughts easily able to alter your mood?

2. During those days when everything seems to go wrong, do the circumstances of your day shipwreck your faith? (i.e. you want to give up on your job, yourself or even God).

3. Do you get bad attitudes about dating when your date has to cancel?

4. Are you excited about building relationships with the lost?

5. When you do not see the results you would like for your efforts, are you known for being the discouraged disciple or the disciple who perseveres?

Being content is deeper than just being an overall happy person. It hinges on how grateful you are to God. The above questions reveal how much or how little you allow gratitude to guard your heart and your mind from the daily attacks of the world. As single disciples, we become discontented, even bitter, because we are not married after a number of years in the kingdom, or we are not holding a certain position in the kingdom. We feel like spiritual paupers when we ought to feel like spiritual kings or queens. Instead let us focus on the promises of God, then we can maintain a grateful attitude that can protect our hearts and minds from the spiritual decay caused by discontentment.

Immeasurable Life
Satan can often cause us to focus on what we do not have so that we forget what God has already given us and vows to give to us in the future. When your heart begins to lose gratitude, remember all that God promises:

- Life to the full (John 10:10)
- An overabundance in return for your sacrifices
      (Malachi 3:10; Luke 6:38)
- To make grace abound (2 Corinthians 9:8)
- To keep you from falling (Jude 24)
- To listen to and answer your prayers
      (Psalm 91:15; Isaiah 65:24; Luke 11:9; John 15:7)
- To give you the desires of your heart
      (Psalm 37:4, 103:5, 145:19)
- To give a fruitful life (John 15:5)

All of this and more, in addition to the Spirit and the for-giveness we were given when we were baptized! Do we really believe these promises? If we do, what reason do we have to be ungrateful? So many times I have heard disciples challenge God with why they had not been given the desires of their hearts. That is scary. We don't know what we are saying. No wonder we are ungrateful! It is at these times that we must allow the Word to disciple our hearts: "Be still, and know that I am God" (Psalm 46:10).

We must stop and remember the sovereignty of God instead of focusing on the satisfaction of attaining a cer-tain something within a certain amount of time. We need the spiritual perspective of Jesus who "for the joy set be-fore him endured the cross" (Hebrews 12:2). The joy for Jesus was not in the agony at Golgotha, but in the knowl-edge that his sacrifice would give mankind a second chance. The joy was in his hope for the future, not in his victory of the moment. We, too, must fight to keep this perspective when we begin to lose our gratitude and doubt God's promises. In order to remain strong we must pull up these bitter roots of discontentment as they take hold and plant the Word in their place. Remember that God promises to give you an immeasurable life of immeasurable impact—if only you will not give up.

Immeasurable Relationships

As we read the Old Testament we see that the people of God would remember him, be grateful and then be blessed by God. With the passage of time, however, they would forget. They would lose their gratitude, harden their hearts and fall from God's grace. After considerable suffering, they would cry out to God, and he would answer them. When we lose our gratitude, we also join the ranks of those who have a "yo-yo" type of relationship with God: up and down, up and down. We can end the cycle if we will identify and prevent those patterns of thinking that steal our gratitude.

Singles, I believe the greatest cause of our discontentment is the struggle with our own singleness. In the Old Testament, we see parallel circumstances, as many men and women wrestled with wanting and waiting for God to bless them with children. By studying the various outcomes of their lives, we can build our own faith as we await the fulfillment of God's promises in our own lives.

> For everything that was written in the past was written to teach us, so that through endurance and the encouragement of the Scriptures we might have hope (Romans 15:4).

I am amazed at how often couples in the Old Testament were not able to have children. Sarah finally had a son at ninety years of age! Rachel, too, was at first barren and became so bitter in her heart that she died in child-birth, naming her final son Ben-Oni, or "son of my trouble." Samson's mother was for a long time sterile and childless; Hannah's womb had been temporarily closed by the LORD. Michal, wife of David, remained childless her whole life. The Shunammite woman bore a son only after Elijah's prophecy. These women and their respective husbands struggled and waited while God used these trials to test and strengthen their hearts, build their characters and teach them gratitude.

In the kingdom today we have a similar challenge. In the same way childlessness tested their hearts, so single-ness tests ours. We struggle and wait. Many of us lose heart, lose gratitude and become bitter. We do so because we have forgotten the immeasurable number and depth of relationships that God has already blessed us with. We become discontented because we haven't learned to be content through our relationship with God, and we don't fully appreciate our incredible relationships with brothers and sisters, married and single. Let us learn a lesson from our predecessors and be grateful for the relationships we already have!

Our most important relationship is with God. He is our friend (John 15:15), Father (John 15:16), Maker (Psalm 95:6) and even spouse (Isaiah 54:5). His love repaired the dam-age in our broken relationship with him. Without him we would not know love. In addition to all this, he gave us each other, the family of believers. What incredible memo-ries I have made with roommates and discipling partners and coleaders over the years. I have a best friend on the other side of the world with whom I had nothing in common when we first met. Now I cannot imagine my life without her. In addition to all this, I have brothers who have sacrificed to take me out and encourage me. I have many spiritual mothers and fathers in the kingdom who have poured their lives into me and loved me even when I was unlovable.

Imagine if you knew about all of this before you became a disciple. After years in the kingdom, have you forgotten the immeasurable gift of relationships? Do not be so busy and distracted that you forget the gifts you have been given as so many did in the Old Testament. Do not have a yo-yo relationship with your Creator. Remember and be grateful. A content heart will always follow.

Immeasurable Power

The power of God—it truly is immeasurable. What we need to understand, however, is that God gives us this same power because we are his children, his heirs. He will strengthen us with power through his Spirit (Ephesians 3:16; 2 Timothy 1:7) and perfect his power in our weakness (2 Corinthians 12:9). As you look deeper, you will find that the power manifesting itself in the disciples is always accompanied by their works of service. The power of Stephen manifested itself as he taught, preached, served and died for the cause of Christ (Acts 6:8-15). In 1 Corinthians 2:4, the "demonstration of the spirit's power" came as Paul preached the message of the cross. Power was also poured out in order to give the disciples endurance and patience as they "bore fruit in every good work"

(Colossians 1:10-11). When we want to tap into the power of God, we must follow these examples and be servants of God by fulfilling his purpose of seeking and saving the lost. As singles, this is the best time in our lives to be filled with the power of God as we devote ourselves totally to our purpose. We need to be grateful that this can be the most powerful time of our lives.

Paul explains this in 1 Corinthians 7:29-35 as he pleads with the disciples to remember that "the time is short" and that "this world in its present form is passing away." He goes on to explain that being married can divide our interests. As singles, we can live "in undivided devotion to the Lord." While not discounting marriage, Paul views singleness as a blessing because it enables us to be consumed with our purpose, able to change the world powerfully. What have you accomplished for God as a single? If you find yourself ungrateful or discontented, you are most likely not embracing your purpose and are not experiencing God's power working through you.

It is time to refocus on our love for people. As we spend ourselves loving others the way God loves them, he will surely watch over our personal cares and concerns, including finding that special someone. As we fight the spiritual battle, he will empower us to persevere through the struggles we face, for "he will be...a source of strength to those who turn back the battle at the gate" (Isaiah 28:6). At a recent singles' conference I heard Randy McKean put it this way, "After you are in the battle, focused on the spiritual war at hand, your perfect match will be the one who is standing right next to you as the smoke clears on the battlefield at the end of a fight." Remembering that illustration has encouraged me to keep my eyes on the battle, knowing that God will take care of my needs as he promised.

This year I have seen some of my best friends, heroes in the faith who have persevered through the battles, find their "perfect match." The smoke cleared, and God blessed them because they kept their focus on God's purpose. They are some of the most powerful disciples I have ever met.

One sister is such an example to me. She became a disciple when she was eighteen years old. She has been fierce about God's purpose for fifteen years as a single disciple, using her singleness to have an impact on hundreds of women. She also had her moments of discouragement, yet she continued to be open about her feelings. She never became bitter about dating, and she gave her heart completely to the brothers. She did not compromise God's standard and always wanted a spiritual mate who would fight the battle with her. As I write these words, she is two weeks away from getting engaged to her perfect match. I know that she will continue to reach many women as a married woman because she developed these convictions while she was single. What power her life shows and what glory her life brings to God! I am honored to know her.

If we remember all the promises of immeasurable life, relationships and power, they will help us in our fight against ingratitude and discontentment. Still, if all these promises were taken away, if all the power was gone, if you were a disciple on your own, would remembering the day and the way Jesus died be enough for you to tough it out? Is his sacrifice on the cross alone able to keep you faithful and grateful to God? Count the cost—again. Then remember why you are who you are and imitate him who "for the joy set before him endured the cross" (Hebrews 12:2).

FOCUS THOUGHT

I have wants, but I am blessed.

7

Conviction with a Dash of Cool

GARY BARBER AND REBECCA OKONKWO

> Our conscience testifies that we conducted ourselves
> in the world, and especially in our relations with you, in the
> holiness and sincerity that are from God.
>
> *2 CORINTHIANS 1:12A*

There is no way I'm going to be Bible Billy, I (Gary) thought to myself as I studied the Scriptures that talked about being a disciple. I knew I needed to be one, but I wanted the loophole—that one word or phrase that would let me off the hook from being a Bible-totin', Scripture-quotin' geek.

I think one of the biggest fears for people desiring to follow God is that they will become a Christian and a geek simultaneously! Out with all my favorite music, clothes and activities—no style, no smile, no fun. People think that God actually wants to ruin their fun, mainly because they just don't see "Christians" having any. People think that it is just not cool to be a Christian.

"Cool" is dictated by the latest and the greatest trend, whether it be fashion, hairstyle, address, activities or connections. Yet for some sad reason when we are in the world, we want it all. Women try so desperately to be pretty or thin to the point of bulimia and bankruptcy. Men have to own all the right toys. These pursuits make us liars and manipulators, cold and arrogant people. We want popularity and identity, but what we get is an empty, dark, shallow, unstable facade—a white-washed tomb.

As disciples, being *in* the world but not *of* the world can be a difficult concept to grasp. Man has spent two millennia trying to reconcile "do not love the world or anything in the world" (1 John 2:15) with "I have become all things to all men" (1 Corinthians 9:22). Jesus prayed for us in John 17:15-16,18,

> "My prayer is not that you take them out of the world but that you protect them from the evil one. They are not of the world even as I am not of it.... As you sent me into the world, I have sent them into the world."

We are supposed to be in the world but not engulfed by the world, cool and full of life (John 10:10) but not flirting with the temptations of the world. We can tend to swing the pendulum from one extreme to the other: Either we live a monastic lifestyle in which we are so separated from people that no one can relate to us or we become so much like the world that no one can tell that we're different. The key here is balance. Remember, fearing God will help us avoid all extremes (Ecclesiastes 7:18).

Jesus gives us the best example of a strong, cool presence. His first miracle was at a wedding (John 2:1) where he was hanging out with his friends and family. After that he cleared a temple with a whip! (John 2:13). Jesus was not only found where the action was, but he was the life of the party. Here are a few thoughts from the two of us that can help you influence the world in your own life.

Shining Like Stars

Do everything without complaining or arguing so that you may become blameless and pure, children of God without fault in a crooked and depraved generation, in which you shine like stars in the universe as you hold out the word of life (Philippians 2:14-16).

God never intended for us to disassociate ourselves from the world; otherwise we would have to leave the world (1 Corinthians 5:9-10). But as we remain in the midst of the world, our lives should bring light to those in darkness.

Stars stand out against the darkness of the night. As disciples, our integrity, purity, love and uncompromising commitment to God should stand out all the more against the backdrop of the world.

Are you a star mistaken for the sky? Do you participate in water-cooler gossip, office flirting or coarse joking? Do you struggle when the unrighteous get ahead or sacrifice what's spiritually important (church, family, relationships) to be competitive with the world? Do people know unmistakably that you are a Christian by your example at home, school or work?

Jesus shows us we can have the fulfilling life of impact, but more importantly, the spirituality it takes to overcome the world and have peace in our hearts (John 16:33). We are sent into the world to influence it, not to be judgmental of it. Ask yourself: Do people see my life as full, fun, focused and righteous? Does the world see real relationships in my life—friendships with men and women that are deep, pure and fun? Are people interested in my life?

When I (Gary) worked at a fashion house as a graphic designer, every Monday morning at 10:00 A.M., the women of my office would ask for a "C.H.A." update. (They affectionately call the kingdom the Church of the Highly Attractive.) They plied me for the details of my weekend date—what we did, with whom and if I was going to go steady with that person. They marveled at the care, the planning and the creativity that went into the dates. Then, they couldn't believe I would send a handmade card to someone I wasn't trying to seduce. They were so familiar with the disciples in my life that they would ask how they were and who they liked and so forth. They were interested in my life because *I had one*, and I invited them in.

Uncompromising Convictions

> Do not love the world or anything in the world. If anyone loves the world, the love of the Father is not in him (1 John 2:15).

This passage is clear—no compromise! What does the world love? Money, sex, beauty, pleasure, fame, power, comfort, etc. The world loves itself. In direct contrast, God loves us and sacrificed his only Son for us. The world loves with stipulations; Jesus loves unconditionally to the full extent (John 13:1).

> For everything in the world—the cravings of sinful man, the lust of his eyes and the boasting of what he has and does comes not from the Father, but from the world (1 John 2:16).

There is a constant craving that is never satisfied in the world. Whether you live in New York, Paris or Jakarta, or one of a thousand other cities, there are thousands of temptations calling out from the television, billboards and news stands saying, "Buy me," "Try me," "Meet me," "Charge me," "Lease me," "Rent me," "Own me," "Steal me," etc. Me, me, me. It is all the world ever talks about. As disciples, we must remember that "the world and its desires pass away, but the man who does the will of God lives forever" (1 John 2:17).

Because of all that goes on around us, we must make sure that we are deeply rooted in the Word. This develops deep conviction and obedience.

> For though we live in the world, we do not wage war as the world does. The weapons we fight with are not the weapons of the world. On the contrary, they have divine power to demolish strongholds. We demolish arguments and every pretension that sets itself up against the knowledge of God, and we take captive every thought to make it obedient to Christ (2 Corinthians 10:3-5).

Setting our minds is not a one-time event, but a training in righteousness. We develop a hatred of sin, which causes us to behave differently.

Before I (Gary) worked in the ministry, I worked in an atmosphere that was fast paced and supercharged due to very tight deadlines. There was also a lot of cursing, and I decided to change it. At first I made little comments like "nice mouth," but it had very little effect. So I singled out the ringleader who just happened to be my boss. One day I picked an opportune time, pulled him aside and had a frank talk with him about what I saw as a lack of leadership in the studio characterized by unprofessional language, temper tantrums and high stress. It was hard to say, and even harder for him to hear, but because he respected my friendship and opinion, he was willing to change. He became the policeman in the studio over the next several weeks and the environment completely changed. People began to admit that they did not like the cursing either. He even began to be interested in the Bible.

The difference between conviction and deep conviction is that conviction is what we live by, but deep conviction is what we are willing to influence others to follow. We do not have to tolerate sin, and our deep convictions can change lives!

Willing to Change

We put no stumbling block in anyone's path, so that our ministry will not be discredited (2 Corinthians 6:3).

Anyone who becomes a disciple would never intentionally hinder someone else from having a relationship with God. But do you realize that being "unrelatable" hinders the gospel? By unrelatable we mean that you're the kind of person who thinks MTV is the chemical sign for Boron. Now wait a minute—it doesn't have to be that silly. For example, maybe you use a lot of "kingdom" language that no one but you and other disciples can understand. If so, you are unrelatable to the majority of people on the face of the earth. This may be hard to accept, but if the pocket protector fits... Paul understood this concept, and it caused him to write,

I have become all things to all men so that by all possible means I might save some. I do all this for the sake of the gospel, that I may share in its blessings (1 Corinthians 9:22-23).

People cannot relate to super-Christians. In fact, the opposite results: Either they give up on God because they can't be like who you are pretending to be, or they find your life so uninteresting that it makes the gospel unattractive.

To what lengths have you gone to impress a man or woman you were romantically interested in? It is not uncommon for people to change hairstyle, weight, clothes or habits. How much more should we be willing to change any aspect of our lives for the gospel that sets us free from the stranglehold of the world! Timothy was willing to be circumcised by Paul just to fit in with the Jews of the area (Acts 16:3). We need to have the same kind of heart—open and willing to change. "I'm not good with people," "That's the way I've always been," "I don't like crowds," and "It doesn't feel natural" are all merely excuses not to change. The Holy Spirit gives us the power to change and be like Jesus. People will be attracted to God if we share what *we* have changed through the power of God rather than what *they* need to change.

'Cool' Practicals
- Home-court advantage—Throw great, creative theme parties (no chips and dip). Practice hospitality (Romans 12:13) rather than put yourself in a worldly environment.
- Do what your friends like to do—It adds variety to your

life, and people appreciate it. Get to know their friends and hobbies. Jesus influenced Levi that way (Luke 5:29).

- Find out what's up—Find out the goings-on about town. There are always interesting things to do for little or no money: jazz festivals, ballroom dancing lessons, live bands. Venture out, be among the people and make new friends!

- Pick up a magazine—Sometimes our appearance can be outdated. Subscribe to a fashion, news or fun magazine. Have someone with taste you admire go through your closet and make suggestions. (This takes guts!)

- Be excellent at something—God gave you talent, personality and interests to use to influence people. Use them to win people. You can even discover new talents you never knew you had like lifting weights, aerobics or dance. Do something, and do it now.

- Be active in the community—Volunteer in some capacity. This is one of the best ways to serve your community and meet people who care about others.

- Be bold—Pray for boldness in every situation. It takes boldness to put your heart out to the people.

Don't the daily newspapers show that the world's answers don't really work? But the one who does God's will, living to please him, is cool. It's cool to be able to wear white on your wedding day and represent your true purity. It's cool to go to sleep at night with a clear conscience. It's cool to have people want to be like you because you are like Jesus—strong, confident, bold, loving, gentle, full of vision and dreams. A hero!

Our hope is that, as your faith continues to grow, our area of activity among you will greatly expand, so that we can preach the gospel in the regions beyond you (2 Corinthians 10:15-16a).

Focus Thought

I am in the world to help people be saved.

8

Dating
in the Kingdom

JIM BROWN AND TERESA DAVIS BROWN

There was silence on the phone. I (Jim) had just asked my mother why it was that I was thirty-six years old and still single. I couldn't tell whether she was praying for wisdom, or if she was just praising God from the bottom of her heart that I had finally asked. Whatever she was doing, the silence seemed to last forever.

I wanted to get married and was eagerly looking for a wife. I had been on hundreds upon hundreds of dates but remained a very frustrated, very single man. I had just started taking Teresa out on dates and was developing a great friendship with her, but there were no fireworks. There was nothing that convinced me that our great friendship was anything more than just that—a great friendship.

Teresa is beautiful, talented, witty and fun. I remember talking with her on the phone and laughing so hard I would fall out of my chair. The only "problem" was that she did not resemble what I had always imagined my wife would look like. You see, although Teresa is beautiful, I had in my mind this list of exact physical features that I expected the woman I married to possess. Without knowing it I had developed a serious case of tunnel vision. What I needed more than anything was someone to set me straight, someone to help me see the whole picture and give me some peripheral vision.

My mother, a disciple of nine years, finally ended the world's longest phone pause by telling me very politely that I was selfish. She said, "You're very focused on *your* mission and what *you* want in a wife, but you're oblivious to these women's true qualities. You need to write these women's qualities down on a piece of paper and pray about it." I did what my mother said, and my convictions changed. Within a matter of days, the way that I viewed women changed. My mother's honesty really helped me; it was true, I was selfish. I was too focused on what *I* wanted in a relationship to be open to God's will for my life. I was too absorbed with worldliness to dream of the godly woman that he had dreamed of for me. I repented, and it was only a few months later that Teresa and I were married!

Men and Love

Brothers, let me give you some profound insight: Despite what you think, you are not a Greek god, so stop looking for that Greek goddess. Come down from Mount Olympus, and get real with yourself—you are not nearly as hot a catch as you think you are.

Men are naturally selfish. Ever since women first caught our eye, we have been compiling a list of what *we* expect our wife to be in order to meet our needs and wants. We cannot imagine spending the rest of our lives with someone who does not measure up to our carefully compiled criteria. When we become disciples, we disguise the list by saying that the most important qualities are spiritual ones, and we leave it at that. Deep down, however, what is most critically important to us are still those physical qualities on "the list."

If this description fits, you really need to get a conviction to change. You are worldly and unspiritual (and the Word warns us against this type of worldliness).

> What causes fights and quarrels among you? Don't they come from your desires that battle within you? You want something but don't get it. You kill and covet, but you cannot have what you want. You quarrel and fight. You do not have, because you do not ask God. When you ask, you do not receive, because you ask with wrong motives, that you may spend what you get on your pleasures.
>
> You adulterous people, don't you know that friendship with the world is hatred toward God? Anyone who chooses to be a friend of the world becomes an enemy of God (James 4:1-4).

God also has a list, but it is very different from ours! Ours is worldly; God's is spiritual. We look at the outward appearance; God looks at the heart. God created marriage, and he is really the only one who knows how it functions. God's list of qualities includes friendship, honesty, openness, serving one another and mutual respect. These things must be the real criteria for us. This is not to say that physical attraction is not important, but it is not as important as you probably think it is.

The fact is that all women are beautiful in God's sight. Whether a woman is short or tall, blonde or brunette, dark or light—physical "specs" do not matter to God. God views them all as gorgeous. You need to reorient your thinking and stop limiting yourself to one particular "type" of woman. You will end up being blind to the woman that God created to meet your needs.

Why is it that some men in the world get divorced from stunningly beautiful women? These women's looks have not changed. They still have the look of a *Vogue* model, yet their husbands are divorcing them. Why? There is more to a good marriage than outward beauty and sex. These men were obviously focused on outward things; therefore the marriage failed.

The Bible defines love, not in terms of feelings or emotions, but in terms of commitment. You will not find a single "feeling" word in 1 Corinthians 13, the most famous definition of love in the Bible. Great marriages are built on a foundation of selflessness, trust and respect. Most of what you *feel* can easily be shattered within moments by unfortunate circumstances. True love is an action, not a feeling.

Face it: You don't know what is going to make you happy—God does. So stop seeking women that meet the qualifications of *your* list, and start seeking women who meet the qualifications on *God's* list. Burn the worldly list today!

The Date

The world says that chivalry is dead, but it is not dead in the kingdom! On the contrary, what makes dating so special in the kingdom is that we honor one another above ourselves. We need to serve our sisters in a very special way through dating.

Our sisters are being constantly romanced by men in the world. They open doors for them, compliment the way they are dressed, tell them how beautiful they are, give them cards and flowers, etc. Sisters are constantly being asked out on dates by worldly men, but because they are disciples, they say no. It is not always an easy victory, however; this is a serious battle. It is not easy to just say no if dates in the kingdom are nonexistent or not excellent and if worldly men act with more kindness and chivalry than the brothers do.

If we, as men of God, saw with the spiritual eyes that we needed to, this would not be an issue. What I mean is this: If you saw someone *physically* attacking your mother or your biological sister or daughter, trying to hurt them, you would be filled with rage and would immediately do whatever you could to protect them. There is a very real threat against our sisters, and as brothers who are warriors in God's army, we must take responsibility for protecting them. The fight is real. See it. There should be no difference between the seen and the unseen realm for the man who follows Jesus.

You need to date your sisters. It should shame you to know that there are men in the world who treat your sisters better than you do. So let's repent and treat our sisters with the honor they deserve. "Be devoted to one another in brotherly love. Honor one another above yourselves" (Romans 12:10).

The 7 Habits of Spiritual Single Brothers

I was baptized as a college student at twenty-two and dated for twelve years as a single in the kingdom. Because of the literally hundreds upon hundreds of dates that I have been on in the kingdom and because of the mistakes I have made and the victories I have experienced, let me share some practical, spiritual advice about dating with you.

1. Date Often

In most cases it is impossible to be an effective discipler of men (or disciple-maker) if you are not consistently dating women. Most men in most cultures today would not want to imitate a man who does not date. It would seem that few have the gift Paul described in 1 Corinthians 7:7.

Also, the more you date, the more sisters get served, the more you learn how to be a better friend to women, and the more equipped you will be to start looking for a wife. We will all end up with only one woman, but as a result of great Christian dating, we will end up with scores of great friends who are women, as well.

The fact is that Jesus had many great friendships with women. They were constantly serving him and meeting his needs because he treated them very well. Jesus treated women with such a total respect and love that he won the hearts of many he came in contact with. As men who claim to follow him, we must be like him and have many great friendships with our sisters. It is simply a matter of being spiritual. It is simply a matter of being like Jesus. God will not bless you with a great wife if you don't first learn how to be a great brother to his daughters.

2. Plan the Date

One of the most insulting things you can do to a woman is to show up for a date and say, "Uh, I don't know. So, what do you want to do?" What it really says is, "I don't care about you. You're not special. I'm only doing this because I have to."

In order for sisters to feel special, they need to see that you have spent time thinking about your time with them, that you have fully planned it. They need to know what is going on in advance. For example, what time are you going to pick her up, and what time are you going to bring her back? Where are you going? What are you doing? How should she dress? Does she need to bring anything with her? Being told these things gives her the security of knowing that you care.

3. Look Sharp

As brothers who care, we need to look our best for our sisters. A few (extremely important, often overlooked!) tips: Shower. Shave. Wear deodorant. Carry breath mints or gum. Iron the clothes you are going to wear. And unless your date is allergic to such things, wear cologne.

Proverbs 11:14 says, "For lack of guidance a nation falls, but many advisers make victory sure." The wise man seeks advice in every area of his life. Appearance should be no exception. Seek advice from brothers who do look their best. Your standard should be to look as good as you possibly can with what you have. If you can look like you walked out of a *GQ* magazine, you will certainly make an impression. Look your absolute best! Not only will she feel great about the date, but you will feel confident yourself.

4. Confirm the Date

As many brothers have erroneously done, *never* show up at her door Saturday at 7:00 P.M. if the last time you talked to her about the date was a month ago. Dates must be confirmed. Call her several days before the date confirming all the details about your plans and say something like, "I'm certainly looking forward to our time together." Then call her the day before, reconfirming what you confirmed several days earlier. This will ensure that there is no confusion and makes a great impression.

5. Be a Gentleman

Some brothers treat their cars with more respect than the sisters they take out. That is not very chivalrous! What do I mean by chivalry, anyway? It means treating a woman like a princess. Open doors for her (yes, car doors too!). Pull out her chair for her at the table, and push it back in. Allow her to order first, then you order. Excuse yourself if you leave the table or her presence. Stand up if a woman, or anyone for that matter, enters. Introduce her to people. Give her a flower, send her a card, give her a small gift—or all three. Find out something that she likes, and get it for her. Bottom line: Honor her.

6. Get to Know Her

Men grow close through activities. Women grow close through sharing. The best dates are those that successfully combine great activities with special time to just talk. Be open and vulnerable on your date. Share with her what is special to you, and find out what is special to her. Do this and you will be on your way to developing a great friendship. In other words, just taking her to a party is not going to cut it.

If you are at a large activity (like a party, or a thirty-couple tie date), make sure that you focus on your date. Don't be glued to her, but don't get lost in the crowd either. Share the experience with her. It is important that after the function you go somewhere to talk. An all-time favorite is going out for coffee and dessert after a party. Whatever you do, just make sure that you get to spend quality time together.

7. Pay the Bill

A great friend of mine, J.P., an intern in the New York City Church, told me that in his seven years as a disciple (he was converted as a teen), he has never missed a single week without having had a date. Moreover, he has also never allowed any sister to pay for any part of the date. (Yes, he even pays for subway tokens!) He says that he wants the sister he is on a date with to feel special, and he wants her to understand that he is honored to take her out. "I guess I'm old-fashioned, but I just believe it's wrong, and ungentlemanlike to not pay for your date. I want my date to feel like a princess because she is one—she is God's daughter. This is something which I never compromise on, even when the sister asks me to let her help pay. I tell her, 'Thanks, but I'd like to pay.'"

In grave contrast to this, one sister, who is also a close friend of mine, overheard what J.P. was saying and began to tell me horror stories about many of her dates before she married her husband (a dashing devotee of the seven habits). Brothers used to show up at her door late and literally have no plan at all. "So what do you want to do? Maybe we could just walk around." The "dates," if they can even be called that, were planned in the evening, and the sister inevitably would become hungry, having expected to eat dinner together. After waiting for the brother to make some kind of initiative in that direction, she would finally ask, "Could we maybe get something to eat?"

"Oh, I'm sorry. I didn't bring any money. Could you pay for me?" would be the typical reply.

The frightening thing is that what I have just described had not merely been an isolated incident but has happened repeatedly with many different brothers. It really is beyond my comprehension how anyone could treat his sister, God's daughter, in such a way. Brothers, this must not happen. Be a gentleman; lead the way; pay for your date!

The Conclusion of the Matter
> He who pursues righteousness and love
> finds life, prosperity and honor (Proverbs 21:21).

A Knight in Shining Armor

So you want to marry a princess? Then you need to be a prince. Think about everything that you dream of and long for—and now reverse it on yourself. You want a wife who respects you? Then become worthy of respect. You want a wife who is beautiful? Then get in shape. You want a wife who is spiritually strong? Then get strong yourself, so you will truly be able to lead her.

You know what your dreams are, but what do the sisters dream of? They dream of a knight in shining armor sweeping them off their feet. It is time that you become that knight. They dream of marrying a man who loves God with all his heart. They dream of a man who wants to present his bride radiant before God. It is time that you fulfill your potential and become that man. It is time to polish your armor.

You may have been convicted by some points, or every point, in this chapter. You may even feel like I wrote this article about you personally and want to go hide in a cave. Well, don't! Get back here! Stand up! Be a man! Put on your armor and polish it! Put these habits into practice, and you will shine before God.

Every man wants to be a hero, and the time to be one is now, not only to the lost, but to the saved as well. God will honor the man who honors his daughters. Let us burn our worldly lists and lay down our lives for our sisters.

Brothers, *polish your armor!* And just watch what God will do.

If You Want the Perfect Man, Follow *the* Perfect Man

> This is how we know what love is: Jesus Christ laid down his life for us. And we ought to lay down our lives for our brothers.
>
> *1 JOHN 3:16*

It all started when I (Teresa) fell in love with Jesus. What a man! My standard of the perfect boyfriend changed dramatically, so I began my dating quest for the "perfect man." This quest required scrutiny, since my mission was to calculate and evaluate each date's potential as my future husband. My mental tabulation (cerebral spouse-o-meter) began before the doorbell rang:

Hmm, fifteen minutes late—not good. (The door opens.) Well, at least he's a sharp dresser—good. No flowers—not good. He has detailed plans for the date—good. At a seafood restaurant—not good. He's athletic—good. He hates my favorite music, and he can't sing a note—not good. He has a sense of humor—good. His favorite words are "awesome" and "fired up"—not good.

Get the picture? With such a critical eye, no man can pass your examination.

If you want the perfect man, then follow the perfect man. In our efforts to find a Christlike man, we often neglect to imitate Christ ourselves. You want perfection in a man. Are you a perfect woman? When we date "looking for a husband," we are centrally focused on what he can give us. Jesus, however, says that it is more blessed to give than to receive (Acts 20:35). Jesus, the one and only *perfect* man, focused on giving in his relationships. When we decide to be like Jesus on our dates—to serve, to encourage, to listen, to evangelize, to be a friend—then our dates will be a blast. Otherwise, we will inevitably return home after our dates feeling unfulfilled and disappointed.

The success of our dating life, therefore, does not depend on who we date or how often we date, but rather on our commitment to imitating Christ in all circumstances. We must lay down our lives for our brothers.

Follow Advice

The way of a fool seems right to him,
> but a wise man [or woman] listens to advice
> (Proverbs 12:15).

When we become Christians, we clearly see our need for advice in our daily lives; however, we often fail to see as clearly our need for advice when it comes to Christian dating. There are no "dating rules" per se; the only rules are God's rules of purity and righteousness. So you say, "Then why do I need advice?" In 1 Corinthians 6:12 Paul says, "Everything is permissible for me, but not everything is beneficial." There are often dating practices that are not wrong biblically speaking, but they are not what is best. For example:

- *Is it wrong to be alone with a brother in your apartment?* The Bible is silent on that, but experienced Christians have learned through the years that it is not best. It is a temptation opportunity.
- *Is it wrong to aggressively pursue the brother that you have a crush on? To call him seventeen times a week? To flood him with weekly brownies, cookies and cards?* It is not beneficial for you or him, unless you prefer that he flee from you screaming with his arms flailing. Just learn to be his friend. Be secure and patient.
- *Is it wrong to talk on the phone every night with a brother after midnight?* In many cases it proves detrimental to one or both person's fight for purity.

There are innumerable things that we do not know about how to meet a brother's needs. If your goal in dating is to be the best friend to the brother that you can be, then don't be a fool and think that you know the way to do that. Get advice from mature, spiritual sisters who are exemplary in their relationships with brothers, and then, of course, follow the advice.

Follow the Brothers

Do not let any unwholesome talk come out of your mouths, but only what is helpful for building others up according to their needs, that it may benefit those who listen (Ephesians 4:29).

God established that men must lead women in Christian relationships. Our pride often causes us to believe that we know better than God, because we think that we know better than the brothers. We get on our high horse spiritually and decide to ride heroically into the brother's life and rescue him from his sin. Then dates become discipling times—bad move! If you want to strengthen the brothers, then build them up. Find their strengths and express them. This will benefit them much more than you teaching them.

Occasionally, you will see weaknesses in a brother. Trust God and trust other brothers to disciple these weaknesses and to help him to overcome. If you have any serious concerns, seek advice on how to approach the situation.

One of women's biggest gripes is that they wait for the brothers to lead in the setting up of dates, but then the brothers do not ask sisters out and we get upset. I think that these attitudes are sparked by our insecurity: If we are asked out, then we feel more attractive, more secure. It is time to get our security from God and let go of the issue of who asks whom on dates. If that means that we set up every single date we have, then so be it. I personally preferred doing the asking because it meant that I could fill my book with dates that I was eager to have. Once you get a date, ask him if he would like to plan it or if he would like you to plan it. Let him decide. Let him lead. (Note: If you ask a brother out and you plan the date, be prepared to pay for part or all of the date. If he insists on paying, then be sensitive about the cost of the date you have planned.)

It is much easier to follow our brothers' lead once we have learned how to have great friendships with them. Let's face it—as disciples, our schedules get so crazy that if we do not date frequently, then our relationships with brothers may suffer. I must emphasize the importance of frequent dating. Sisters who date frequently are rarely, if ever, tempted with worldly men, because when they are surrounded by godly men who are their best friends, worldly men cannot even hold a candle to them. Go out of your way to make your dating life happen.

Follow the Most Excellent Way

Your beauty should not come from outward adornment, such as braided hair and the wearing of gold jewelry and fine clothes. Instead, it should be that of your inner self, the unfading beauty of a gentle and quiet spirit, which is of great worth in God's sight (1 Peter 3:3-4).

Often women use the above passage as an excuse to compromise in their physical appearance. We puff ourselves up through our spiritual beauty, confident that if a man is truly spiritual, he will fall in love with our heart, regardless of how we look physically. The fact is, our outward appearance is a reflection of our heart. It may expose our laziness and our rebellion toward God's high standard.

We live in an age when physical appearance is what the world respects. Health clubs, jogging, roller blading and super models are all indicators of the world's priorities. Paul said in 1 Corinthians 9:22, "To the weak I became weak, to win the weak. I have become all things to all men so that by all possible means I might save some." Forget the dating issue for a minute and understand that we may hamper our effectiveness as Christians in the world because of our stubborn refusal to become whatever we need to be to win those people. If you want to save this world, do not give them an excuse to disrespect you before they even hear your message. We must prove ourselves excellent both spiritually and physically in order to bring glory to God.

Get an objective opinion from a close friend. Tell them to be painfully honest with you about your appearance. I am thankful that I did. I learned that my wardrobe, my make-up and my body all needed to change. My first reaction was, "But this is just me." Trust the people in your life when they tell you that "me" isn't cutting it. When we signed up to follow Jesus, we signed up to crucify that "me." Open your heart to learn and change whatever will make you look your best for God, for the lost and for your brothers. I had to humble myself and realize that as much as I thought that I knew how to pick clothes and how to do my make-up, I was not doing the best job. I was so encouraged by the floods of compliments I received after I followed the advice of my trusted friends. Then I felt more secure and confident in every area of my life.

Stop making excuses like the following:

- "I'm trying to lose weight, but I'm just too busy with Bible studies and work to exercise," you may say with prideful disdain as you munch down two slices of pepperoni pizza, an ice-cream bar and a Diet Coke.
- "I can't afford new clothes." This may be true, but find someone with the talent to go through your closet and find solutions with what you have.
- "I don't like wearing make-up." Give it a try! Experiment. Have it done professionally at a department store. You will soon like it when you hear the vast accolades from the brothers and sisters who see the improvement.

The Conclusion of the Matter

Do nothing out of selfish ambition or vain conceit, but in humility consider others better than yourselves. Each of you should look not only to your own interests, but also to the interests of others (Philippians 2:3-4).

The bottom line is—if you imitate Jesus' selfless serving heart when it comes to dating, then your dating life will be richly rewarding. Set your mind to love your brothers like Christ, being more concerned with how to meet their needs than your own. If you want the perfect man, follow the perfect man.

FOCUS THOUGHT

Dating in the kingdom is a privilege.

The Bitter Woman

TERESA DAVIS BROWN

"For I see that you are full of bitterness and captive to sin."
ACTS 8:23

Flutter, flutter went my heart as I sat in the cardiologist's office awaiting the diagnosis. Months of heart palpitations mixed with shortness of breath had led me to believe the worst: heart disease. The cardiologist then said to me, "Are you going through a difficult time in your life right now?"

I wanted to scream, "Difficult time? Difficult time?! You better believe it, buddy!" Instead, I said in my most Jesus-like voice, "Somewhat." I left his office furious, knowing that my condition was a result of my sin: stress, bitterness and discontentment.

I did not want to repent because in my mind I had every right to be angry at God. Difficult time? I had been a Christian for six years. I had probably had at least 400 dates with approximately 200-250 different brothers. I had fallen in love at least ten times, and each of those brothers dated me consistently, along with one other sister, until they could "choose" their girlfriend—and they always chose the other girl.

I was swimming in insecurity and loneliness, plagued with questions like, *What's wrong with me? Am I so unattractive? Does God want me to stay single the rest of my life?*

What was worse were the bitter resentments toward God that hardened my heart: "God, how could you do this to me? I've been a Christian six years, and I deserve a husband. Why is it that all these young Christians end up with boyfriends before me? It's not fair! If one more person asks me who I'm interested in, I'm going to scream! (It always happens at weddings.) There is no man in the kingdom for me. I need a break, a vacation. I'm so unhappy."

Satan was having a field day in my heart. I was filled with stress, bitterness, anger, rage, jealousy, discontentment, ingratitude and criticalness of all the brothers—who at this point could do no right. All of these sins combined probably lent themselves to making me the most unattractive sister in the church. It was no coincidence that this was the exact time worldly men began to pursue me. I started getting the attention I desired, because Satan will pay any price for a soul. I also began to justify episodes of masturbation. I had decided that I had a right. It also seemed like every date that I did set up with a brother was either canceled, unplanned and horrible, or he stood me up—just another way that Satan toyed with my heart.

Does any of this sound familiar? If so, it is time to have a radical change in your life, from the inside out. In Acts 8:23 Peter told Simon the Sorcerer, "For I see that you are full of bitterness and captive to sin." That was me. Once we allow a bitter root to make its home in our heart, it sprouts up into every variety of sin until at last we become a slave to Satan and all of his whims.

On that day, when I saw the spiritual condition of my heart, I was forced to my knees in prayer. Through prayer God humbled me, softening my heart. He instilled in me a realization that I had become so ungrateful that it was as if I was looking up at Jesus on the cross and telling him, "It is not enough for you to die for me—I want a husband, and then I'll be happy." I begged for God's forgiveness, and I resolved in my heart to change.

First, I had to repent in my relationship with God. I had become so distant from him emotionally that it was hard for me to read the Bible or pray. I made a decision to make my time with God my food in the morning before anything else entered my mouth. I decided to study out trust in God so that I could get the encouragement that I needed in my faith.

Second, I had to repent of my distrust of God's plan for my life. The scripture that helped me the most was Romans 4:18-21, which says that against all hope, Abraham believed. It looked hopeless. There were no brothers in sight for me to marry, and yet I had to believe that God would bless me. So often when we face the facts like, "I'm thirty years old. I've dated everyone I can think of, and no one is interested in me," those facts steal our faith. I decided to imitate Abraham's trust. He waited much longer than six years to see God's promise fulfilled in his life!

Third, I had to decide to be content. Proverbs 19:23 says, "The fear of the Lord leads to life: Then one rests content, untouched by trouble." I realized that all I really need is God. If Jesus were the only partner I ever had in this life, it was more than most women ever dreamed of. God is the only cure for loneliness and misery; a husband is not. I realized that even if I had a husband, our relationship would fall apart if I was not walking with the Lord.

When I got my heart right and let go of the pressure of finding a husband, I began to enjoy dating again, because I did not go on each date with a measuring list (the "spouse-o-meter"!) to see if he measured up to marriage. I decided to just give to and encourage my brothers. It was during this joyful time of renewal with God and heartfelt repentance that God sent Jim Brown home to New York City from Africa. We became best friends and one year later we were married. If he had come home one month earlier, it may not have worked out because he probably would have been under my critical, bitter scrutiny—my sin would have put him off. I thank God for his perfect plan and timing for each of us!

Looking back on those ten brothers who broke my heart, and looking now at Jim, it is so clear that God picked just the right man for me. If I had had to wait ten more years for Jim, knowing what I know now, I would have! We all need to trust our Daddy in heaven.

FOCUS THOUGHT

I will believe this today:
"And my God *will* meet *all* your needs
according to his glorious riches
in Christ Jesus."
(Philippians 4:19, emphasis added)

10

Scaling the Walls of Fear

STEVE TETRAULT

> For God did not give us a spirit of timidity, but a spirit of power, of love and of self-discipline.
>
> *2 TIMOTHY 1:7*

In June 1991 after I was asked to lead the campus ministry at my school, I thought I was going to die. Crumbling with fear and insecurity, I thought *surely* there must be some mistake. My response was not unlike that of Moses. When he was handpicked by God to rescue the Israelites from slavery in Egypt, his response was,

> "O Lord, I have never been eloquent, neither in the past nor since you have spoken to your servant. I am slow of speech and tongue.... Please send someone else to do it" (Exodus 4:10, 13).

Instead of approaching God's calling with feelings of honor and excitement, Moses became overwhelmed with insecurity and dread. He lost his senses, evidently believing that God's judgment was lacking because he *obviously* was unable to do what God thought he was more than capable of accomplishing.

I had always greatly admired people who were confident and secure. I hated living in fear and uncertainty, doubting myself and believing everyone was more spiritual and more talented than I was. I desperately longed for the day when things would be different, when fear and lack of confidence would no longer dominate my life.

Since that day, God has given me a beautiful wife, a child on the way and a region to lead in his church. My life and my character have dramatically changed, and God has been with me every step of the way. If it happened to me, it can happen to you. In my own battle with fear and insecurity, I have found five keys that help us overcome.

Selflessness

For a long time I saw insecurity and lack of confidence as my lot in life: character flaws that I could not change because I was born insecure. I believed that a refusal to be outgoing and expressive was selfish, and therefore sinful, but I was convinced that my "inborn" insecurities *caused* me to be selfish. Repentance of selfishness was therefore optional. The biblical lesson I had to learn was that the opposite was true: I was insecure because I was selfish. When I repented of the selfishness, when I decided to be outgoing and giving, looking to meet the needs of others and not my own needs, I saw fear and lack of confidence quickly diminish from my character.

Proverbs 22:13 reads, "The sluggard says, 'There is a lion outside!' or, 'I will be murdered in the streets!'" Sluggards are people who do nothing but focus on themselves. This leads to fear. When I feel insecure, it is because I am thinking about *me: How am I coming across? What will they think of me? Am I dressed right?* There is a big world out there filled with people with incredible needs, so we all need to focus our attention on somebody other than ourselves. We cannot allow insecurity to be an excuse for being selfish!

Furthermore, insecurity by definition alone is sin. A person who is insecure fails to find security in God. Psalm 112:1, 7-8 describes the man who finds confidence in the Lord:

> Blessed is the man who fears the LORD,
> who finds great delight in his commands.
> ...he will have no fear of bad news;
> his heart is steadfast, trusting in the LORD.
> His heart is secure, he will have no fear;
> in the end he will triumph over his foes.

We must put all of our trust in God, getting confidence from him alone, not from our talents, circumstances or the approval of others. Whenever I try to preach, lead a Bible study, share my faith or talk to others in fellowship without praying about it and putting my trust in God, I feel overwhelmed and powerless. We must "pray in the Spirit on all occasions" (Ephesians 6:18) in order to be secure, confident and effective as disciples. "Self-confidence" is sin; God's desire is for us to get our confidence from him alone.

Spirituality

When God called Gideon, he referred to him as a "mighty warrior," though he was simply a winepress boy who had never been involved in battle. If you are a Christian, God automatically sees you as "perfect" (Hebrews

10:14). God chooses to forget your shortcomings and "remembers your sins no more" (Isaiah 43:25). One of Satan's best strategies is to get us to focus on difficulties, weaknesses, sins and problems. When we lose sight of how God views us, our confidence is destroyed, battered down by negativity, ingratitude and worldly thinking. Keeping God's view of us at the forefront of our minds will help us to walk confidently through life as a disciple.

Transparency

> The man of integrity walks securely,
>> but he who takes crooked paths will be found out
>> (Proverbs 10:9).

Secure people are people who are open with their sin, willing to talk about their weaknesses and eager to get the help needed to strengthen their relationship with God. Insecure people often have hidden, unconfessed sin and invest a great deal of time maintaining a facade that they have created. They make every effort to impress others, yet "make no effort to obtain the praise that comes from the only God" (John 5:44). Insecurity feeds on "unopenness." When we are not vulnerable and transparent with sin, attitudes and weaknesses, we add to the list of fears that are already in our lives the fear of being found out and exposed.

Be willing to look bad in front of others. Don't concern yourself with what people may think about you. As a young disciple, I feared being honest. I wanted to present myself as strong and righteous, especially when I was weak and sinful. This hindered my relationship with God and my relationships with others, and it made me incredibly insecure.

Sadly, many single disciples take a long time to decide to marry because they do not allow anyone to get close enough for fear of baring their weaknesses to another person. I can remember my second date with Tricia, a sister who had sparked my interest, and the decision I made to open up to her about fears I had and insecurities that had plagued me. I daringly (and nervously) bared my soul to her, telling her that I had low self-esteem because I was shorter than most guys and because in the near future I might show up in a "Hair Club for Men" ad. To this she affectionately replied, "Hair doesn't make the man." Two years later she married me.

Diligence

I was unfruitful, unstable and unhappy. I wanted to become secure, confident and effective, but it was impossible for me to change my weak character—impossible until I *decided* to tackle my insecurities and selfishness by faith. I began a fast that would last indefinitely, until people told me they noticed a radical change in my character. I worked hard to be a giver, not a taker, when around others and to be expressive and encouraging. I prayed diligently and begged God to change my selfish character. The fast ended on the eleventh day when two people individually approached me and told me how much they thought I had changed.

Don't listen to Satan's lies when he tells you that you cannot change, and don't become discouraged if you feel as though you are not changing as quickly as you would like. If you truly want your character to change, you must embrace the inevitable suffering and hard work that accompanies it, "because we know that suffering produces perseverance; perseverance character; and character hope" (Romans 5:3-4).

In Luke 18 Jesus told his disciples the parable of the persistent widow "to show them that they should always pray and not give up." Diligent prayer and perseverance are necessary in building your character; don't look for the "quick fix" changes—be determined and trust that God will transform you into someone who is secure, confident and selfless.

Courage

> What the wicked dreads will overtake him;
>   what the righteous desire will be granted
>   (Proverbs10:24).

This verse talks about the consuming nature of fear: The person who dreads will eventually be overtaken by his fears. During the entire time of our engagement, I waited in fearful expectation of the wedding day: *What if I fainted? What if I blanked during my vows? What if I started babbling?* For nearly four months I was overtaken by fear, until evangelist Jim Brown comforted me, "If God wants to humble you [on that day], he will. It's out of your hands, so don't worry about it."

Fear becomes sin when we become enslaved by it, when we spend too much time worrying about what *might* happen. I have often felt fearful before speaking publicly, leading Bible studies or sharing my faith, but by putting my trust in God (and not in myself) in these situations, I have not allowed those fears to control me. It is much easier to not take risks in life—to play it safe, never venturing beyond what you think you can do because of a fear of failure—than to step out on faith, risking looking foolish and becoming discouraged if things do not go as planned. It is easier to duck out and hide in the shadows of the kingdom, never achieving great things for God. Do not look at past defeats and "limitations" in your character, because the God who created the universe, who raised Jesus from the dead, who created you, knows no limitations.

Conclusion

God graciously gave you his Holy Spirit the day you decided to give your life to him and were baptized. Since "God did not give us a spirit of timidity, but a spirit of power, of love and of self-discipline" (2 Timothy 1:7), your *life* must reflect these fruits. Living a life of security and confidence is not an ideal, but a necessity in your walk with the Lord.

In order to become confident and fearless, you must first realize that insecurity is *sin* that is kept alive by selfishness. Repent of any hint of selfishness in your life. Decide to work and pray diligently, and be transparent, not spending your energy looking for man's approval, but realizing that you are *already* approved by God. Since God specializes in turning weakness into strength, we no longer have excuses but opportunities. Allow God to help you scale the walls of fear and insecurity, and live a life of power and confidence!

FOCUS THOUGHT

I will focus on *others* today,
not on me and my fears.

11

Want to Change the World? First Change Your Sheets!

BY GARRY W. VERMAAS AND JODI DOUGLAS

"Let your 'Yes' be yes, and your 'No,' no, or you will be condemned."

JAMES 5:12

Learning in the business world to always be early, I (Garry) knocked on the door of a Manhattan apartment to pick up my date at 6:45, fifteen minutes before she was expecting me. My date, not being ready, asked me to wait patiently on the couch. Thinking about getting to the 7:30 party which was an hour's drive from where we were, I became frustrated. I sat alone waiting, as I do in my dentist's office, for my date and the other sister I was bringing to the party. The next time I glanced at my watch, with sisters popping in and out as I waited, the time was 7:45.

At this point, the other sister decided to go to the grocery store. She asked me to pick her up outside the grocery store three blocks away when my date was ready, so that she could do her shopping and not waste any time. *Maybe she is going to pick up a pack of gum, or perhaps a card for her date,* I thought.

Twenty minutes later (8:30), I was sitting outside the grocery store waiting with my date for the other sister. Reminder: We were already an hour late, and an hour away. I was thrilled when I finally saw her emerge from the store until I looked down to see three bags in her hands. *Shopping for the week?* I wondered. Realizing at that moment that what she had done was causing us to have to go back to the apartment building, she quickly tried to fix the situation by adding, "I can just leave the groceries in the car so we don't have to go all the way back."

I turned to the sister in amazement and asked, "What's in the bag?" I could not believe the response: Among the contents were chicken and ice cream. Of course we returned to the apartment and put the groceries away. (Another fifteen minutes went by...8:45.)

Finally we were leaving, or so I thought. It turns out that her date was not meeting us at the party, which I had assumed, and that we had to pick him up—in Friday night traffic in the middle of New York City!

At this point I just wanted to go home. We made it down to the brother's apartment, but finding no parking, I let my date run up to get the other brother and told her to meet me around the corner where I could park. After twenty minutes of waiting, I got out of the car to look for them. I could not believe it when I saw them chatting in front of the building. *I guess she didn't catch that part about meeting me around the corner,* I thought.

Finally on our way, we hit traffic out of the city, traffic in the tunnel out of the city and came to a detour on the only road I knew for getting to the party for which, by this time, we were already three hours late.

Four hours after the party had started, we arrived (11:30). We got there in time to hear the few people who were still there talk about what an amazing party it had been. So we went to a diner, where my date "officially" began (midnight...six hours after I had left my house in New Jersey). An hour later I found myself back in the car dropping off everyone at their respective apartments. I arrived home at 3:00 A.M. As I realized that I had to get up for church in three hours, I thought, *Well, maybe she isn't the one.*

Can you relate to anyone in this scenario? Sadly, we are sure you have a few of your own stories to tell. Incidents like this one abound. Sometimes they happen in dating, but sometimes even as we reach out to our friends who are searching for God. Something as seemingly trivial as scheduling can end up delaying or preventing people from knowing God. Why are we singles sometimes so notoriously disorganized? We buy planners and calendars, digital or leather-bound, highlighters and yellow sticky notes. We use beepers, voice mail, call waiting. Everyone has given us advice, sample schedules and their convictions. But for us to truly change, we must have our own deep convictions about what God values.

James 5:12 shows us God's attitude toward keeping our commitments, and he is serious enough to offer condemnation as the alternative to being disciplined. If we take this scripture to heart, it will change our lives. God gives us two simple commands. The first is to "let our 'Yes' be yes." This means that when we agree to do something, be somewhere, drop something off, call someone or meet somewhere, we do it, be there, drop it off, call and keep our commitment no matter what else comes up, barring an emergency. We are to do all this and do it on time, every time. We cannot make any exceptions to this command.

During the 1994-1995 academic year, I (Garry) was at Lehigh University working on a graduate degree, and I lived for the whole year with my best friend, Rod. He is probably the most disciplined person I had ever met, which was one of the reasons we got along so well. I remember many of the times that Rod and I made specific plans a week or two in advance with a specific meeting time. Both he and I would arrive at the meeting place fifteen to twenty minutes early every time. We would then proceed to laugh at ourselves and at how different we were from most people we knew. In fact, all our other friends knew this about us as well and frequently made fun of us.

Despite the teasing, the fact that Rod kept every commitment he ever made with me and was always early taught me to trust him. I have often said that if I were ever caught in some far out place in a lot of trouble and I was only allowed to make one phone call, I would call Rod. Because of Rod's discipline, I developed an immeasurable amount of respect for and trust in him. Presently, Rod lives in Philadelphia and I have not seen him in a couple of months, but if I were to call him and ask him to help me, I know that not only would he be there, but he would be there early.

Some relationships in the church, among people who have devoted themselves to the Bible, do not have half of the trust that Rod and I do in our relationship. How many people do not trust us? How many did not come to church or to study the Bible with us because we arrived late or forgot to call them? What about the people who developed a bad attitude against us because we made them wait, even though we said we would be on time and ready to go? Helping others have a relationship with God is all about the relationships we build with them. We need to see that lack of discipline destroys relationships, rather than have the all too common attitude of "It's no big deal."

When we consider the magnitude of James 5:12, we must also reconsider what we agree to do. This is where the "'no' being no" is important. As disciples, we generally want to serve and use our time to God's glory. In our zeal, however, we sometimes forget to think. We must be reasonable about our schedules, not insisting on being somewhere every other hour, leaving no time for traveling or possible traffic. We cannot overbook ourselves and plan ten events for our day, or we will be late and halfhearted for every one of them. Growing up, my father (Mr. Vermaas) would often quote his favorite proverbs. He had an incredible way of saying exactly what needed to be said with no extra words. So in my father's voice I say, "If you're not going to do something right, don't do it at all!"

We must also realize that we cannot use the standard of excellence as an excuse to not do much at all. We must be busy for God, but not busybodies. Responsibly, thoughtfully, prayerfully, we need to discipline our lives and schedules so as to accomplish the most for God. As singles, we have extra time to serve and need to greatly consider how, by letting our "yes" be yes, and "no" be no, we can bring glory to God in our spiritual lives, at our jobs or schools, and at home.

Spiritually Disciplined: Not an Oxymoron

> Be very careful, then, how you live—not as unwise but as wise, making the most of every opportunity... (Ephesians 5:15-16).

The foundation of our discipline begins with our time with God. This time cannot be compromised, cut short or left until after we have done all the "important" things in our day. On Sunday night, with a piece of paper and pencil, you can draw up a rough outline of your schedule for the week. Always put down your time with God first. If Jesus is Lord of our lives, we do not fit God into our schedules; he is our schedule. Keep your time with God as consistent as possible, using the same time and same place with God, to keep yourself from wasting time or becoming distracted. Read. Pray. Pray through your schedule for the day. Especially pray about your times with non-Christians. Whether you have a set study that day or not, your whole day is an opportunity to make an impact for God.

The next area to plan into our schedules is our time with non-Christians. This is where we must make the most of every opportunity. Do not limit yourself to the one hour you have free after work. Plan who you are having lunch with every day, using that time to make friends at work and school. This is where the foundation for friendship begins. Use the car or bus ride home to meet new people or carpool with a friend. Even if your night is packed, take the fifteen minutes you have while preparing dinner to talk on the phone with one of your new friends. We must remember that Jesus did not just study with people. He lived his life with them, including them in every part of his day. Do not allow yourself to use your busy schedule as an excuse for not being with the people God has put in your path.

As disciples we can get weird about life. We skip meals, do not work out or do not set up dates in order to make time for people studying the Bible with us. And we can get pretty prideful about how "sacrificial" we are for God. Jesus did not do this. Evangelism was a joy for him. Being with the people did not replace his life—it was his life. We should be in shape and eat right and date. But all these activities can include our friends who are not yet disciples. Some of the best friends the two of us have made have been in the gym. We have fun, relating with people in a place where they feel comfortable, and really get to know them. We build relationships and set up times to work out together. Also, we plan to go on double dates with different couples we have met at work or school, letting people into our lives to see God through our dating relationship.

As graduate students who also work in the ministry, we both study our schoolwork with friends from class and take study breaks together, talking about life and building deep friendships. This consistency in spending time with people enables them to open up to us and to God more readily. People respond better when we really care and spend the time to care, rather than when we are just making sure we are meeting our Great Commission duty. And what fun it is when evangelism is about people and not about our legalistic duty!

If we think through our week ahead of time, we will realize how much time God has blessed us with. We need to use every opportunity during our day to let people into our lives. This is our purpose, and God will bless our whole-hearted efforts.

Jesus, Employee of the Month—Every Month

Serve wholeheartedly, as if you were serving the Lord, not men, because you know that the Lord will reward everyone for whatever good he does... (Ephesians 6:7-8).

Jesus did "all things well," and as his disciples, so must we. This goal applies to our work and our schoolwork. God has given us the most amazing and important purpose, but we cannot allow our purpose to be an excuse to be mediocre in every other area of our lives.

I (Garry) had the opportunity to spend a lot of time with a brother who became a very good friend of mine. He was willing to sacrifice anything for the kingdom and his heart was to totally work for God. He had a two-and-a-half hour commute to and from a full-time job in Manhattan, but he would go to every meeting (for Bible discussion group leaders, singing groups, teen devotionals). When he arrived home in the suburbs at 7:00 P.M., he would go directly to a meeting. Getting home at 10:30, he would then make phone calls. Somewhere around 2 A.M., he would retire to his room and fall asleep on the floor. He slept on the floor because for six months he never found time to drive to his parents' house (only forty minutes away) to pick up his mattress. Finally, his parents tried to have a mattress delivered to the apartment, but he was never home to receive it. Every night he got about four hours of sleep on that floor (but at least he did not have to take time in the morning to make the bed!). Needless to say, I was not surprised when his boss caught him sleeping on his desk at work. We must work hard, but we must also work smart, otherwise we undermine our influence.

In order to properly represent Jesus, we must try to excel in everything we do. We are his ambassadors, so when we are undisciplined in our lives, we give people a false impression of Jesus. The disciplined disciple goes to bed on time in order to be awake and aware for work and school. While we may have the occasional late-night study, most of our staying up too late comes from wasting time.

My (Garry's) father owned a construction company, and I often remember his common complaint about his workers. Although he was willing to pay for the work they did, he wished they would give a little more than the bare minimum required. "Minute men" was the term used for workers who showed up five minutes before the job and left the instant they completed their work. No one on the site respected them. As disciples, we cannot be "minute men" or "minute women." We need to arrive at work on time, or early, and stay the whole day. Moreover, by being fifteen minutes early to work, we can show our bosses and co-workers that we care about what we do.

The same standard applies to schoolwork. If we are enrolled at a college or university, we should be at every class on time (and awake) with our work completed. We must not allow patterns of incomplete studying and attendance to continue. Ask yourself this: If your coworkers or fellow students were to tell only one characteristic about your performance at work or school, what would it be? Responsible? Diligent? Hard-working? These are the responses we are looking for, right? Do they describe you?

If not, we can change by becoming wholehearted about everything we do, remembering that God is our boss and/or teacher. Being wholehearted means to fully complete your given tasks. Two years ago I (Jodi) was a full-time student at Columbia University taking seventeen hours, an intern in the ministry and a commuter on the New York City bus lines at least an hour a day on school days. I felt so torn between doing well in school and still accomplishing a lot for God. In addition, I wanted to have time for a strong personal ministry. My roommates especially can attest to how challenging this time of my life was. I would struggle with getting frustrated with my school work, wanting just to focus on the ministry. I remember staying up all night one night trying to complete my twenty-page psychology paper. Around 6:00 A.M. as I was finishing my paper, a computer virus attacked and destroyed all my work. With tears in my eyes, I knew I had to start all over again. In situations like this one, I had to fight to stay faithful and focused. I had to be wholehearted about whatever I was doing at that moment.

When I was studying, I could not allow myself to feel guilty about not answering the phone. I also could not let my mind wander to all the people I was reaching out to. At that moment I had to be one-hundred percent focused on my schoolwork. (There's a principle here for people in the working world, as well.) Then when I was at a worship service or in a study, I could not be worried and distracted about the paper that was due the next day. Having this kind of focus, my commute even proved fruitful. I discovered that a friend from that same psychology class rode my bus home, so God gave me an opportunity to reach out to her.

Too many times we are not wholehearted about one endeavor because another one distracts us from the task at hand. We are busy but get nothing accomplished. Satan loves this! To escape this trap we need only to decide to be totally focused on what we are doing at the moment. Do it with all your heart, and then move on. When I was wholehearted (even when I could not find the energy to finish all of my reading or the time to make all of my phone calls), God still blessed what I was doing because he knew I was giving it my best. Consequently, that semester in school was one of my best, as I made the dean's list. (I even "aced" the psychology paper I had to redo, thanks to God!) As you struggle to be wholehearted, remember that God blesses the effort, not the result. When we rely on him, he enables us to excel and to do "all things well."

How Many Dishes Can You Fit into the Sink?

"In the same way, let your light shine before men, that they may see your good deeds and praise your Father in heaven" (Matthew 5:16).

As disciples and imitators of Jesus, we are called to be servants. Let's get real and discover what serving and "good deeds" in a singles' household include:

- Buying toilet paper for your household.
- Buying milk that day when you use the last drop for your bowl of Cheerios.
- Not taking your roommate's laundry out of the dryer and dumping it on the floor so you can put your own in.
- Making sure to pick up your wet towels off the bathroom floor before your roommate's guests come over.
- Cleaning your dishes so that your roommate does not have to eat out for lack of a clean fork.
- Balancing your checkbook.
- Being the one in your household who initiates paying the phone bill—and then even being the one to find a stamp and mail it.

All of these obvious examples need to be mentioned because as singles, we can be inconsiderate procrastinators (not to mention complete slobs!). We must take responsibility to ensure that our homes are places we are proud to show to our friends. At any moment, we should be able to have someone drop by without making them wait outside while we shove the dirty clothes under the bed. In order to achieve this, we need to spend time with our roommates and decide on responsibilities in the household, especially the payment of bills. Once decided, we cannot procrastinate in the completion of our respective tasks, remembering that "Lazy hands make a man poor, but diligent hands bring wealth" (Proverbs 10:4).[1]

[1] For further study on managing money, see *God & Money*, published by Discipleship Publications International.

My present roommate asked me if I (Garry) would help his friend become more organized. We met one afternoon to go over what I thought were bills. As it happened, we ended up going through about *four months of unopened mail*. To our dismay, one of the first letters we opened, postmarked months earlier, was a notice that a dear friend of his had died. Because of his lack of discipline, he not only was delinquent in paying his bills, but also missed an opportunity to minister to a grieving family.

Being irresponsible hurts people. Therefore, we cannot be slow to change. This is also true in our relationships with our immediate families. We must be disciplined enough to call our parents regularly and to spend quality time with them if possible. Since I have become a disciple, this has meant even more to my mom. Staying close to her has shown her that the changes I have made as a disciple are only drawing us closer. Our relationship is the best it has ever been. But all too often, we make the mistake of missing family birthday parties or Mother's Day celebrations for more "spiritual" reasons that we should have been responsible enough to schedule at another time. By doing so, we alienate our families, even slightly, from us and from their chance at seeing God in us.

God states explicitly in the parable of the talents (Matthew 25) that if we are responsible with small tasks, we will be responsible with large ones. We all desire to make an impact for God, but are you disciplined enough for him to trust you with someone's soul? If we dream of returning souls to God, understand that it begins with returning our phone messages. If we have a passion for changing the world, let us start with changing our sheets. Only when we conquer our lack of discipline can God help us to conquer our part of the world!

Discipline with Our Finances

The following input about having discipline with our finances is given by Madaline Evans:

Most people associate discipline with money or weight. It's interesting that a lack of money always makes us feel heavier, weighed down, burdened. The Bible warns that a borrower is servant to the lender (Proverbs 22:7) and commands that we leave no debt outstanding (Romans 13:8). Spending more than we have is not only foolish, but an indication of greed (1 Timothy 6:9). The sooner we realize that a lack of discipline with our finances is sin, and the sooner we take the necessary steps for repentance, the sooner we will reap the harvest of righteousness:

> Consider the blameless, observe the upright;
>   there is a future [posterity] for the man of peace
>   (Psalm 37:37).

In working in financial administration for the church, I inevitably end up counseling a lot of people about their finances. The hardest thing for people to accept (until it chokes them) is that what they see about their finances is real. It is alive, it is out of control, and it is slowly killing them. My motto has always been, "What you see, is." Your eyes do not lie. You can rationalize, fantasize, explain or complain, but the financial picture is still the same. If you are on empty, you are on empty!

The best advice I can give anyone whose finances are out of control is to turn themselves in. Entrust your financial decisions to someone more knowledgeable and disciplined than you. Our lack of discipline generally has little to do with how much we make, but rather how we spend it! Humble yourself, and let someone put you on a budget. Let them teach you how to spend what you do have.

I advise people to complete a budget worksheet in which they list all their living expenses and *all* their debt, including money owed to friends and family. After asking a lot of questions to ensure that the list is complete, I explain how much a family of their size needs to live on. The remainder is used to facilitate their getting out of debt. I explain the difference between good debt (loans for education, automobiles or homes) and bad debt (multiple Visa cards that are maxed-out, bank overdraft protection used monthly to cover what your paycheck won't, etc.). The former is a necessary part of life; however, it should enable you to do more with your life. The latter is a clear indication that your spending habits are out of control.

I strongly urge people to cut up their credit cards, stop using their ATM cards, get a checking account and pay as many bills as possible with a check. It is best to carry as little cash as possible and *only* what is needed for the day. We should set aside our contribution before we pay anything—even our rent. God blesses discipline and expects us to give back to him what he has so freely given us.

Light is shed upon the righteous
and joy on the upright in heart (Psalm 97:11).

This scripture describes the most surprising result in people who begin to stay on their budgets: They feel lighter and have more joy. I believe God blesses them because of their obedience by providing them with additional sources of income, even in the form of debt cancellation. Once we reap the harvest of discipline with our finances, we begin to sow seeds of discipline in other areas of our lives as well.

FOCUS THOUGHT

The word "discipline" and the word "disciple" have a lot in common.

12

Across All Boundaries

JAMES W. MCPHERSON AND MICHELE VAUGHN

When the Samaritan came to draw water, Jesus said to her, "Will you give me a drink?"...

The Samaritan woman said to him, "You are a Jew and I am a Samaritan woman. How can you ask me for a drink?" (For Jews do not associate with Samaritans.)

JOHN 4:7-9

I (James) grew up on the south side of Chicago, not too far from the Muslim temple where Louis Farrakhan would speak. I can still hear the voice of my uncle (a former Black Panther turned Muslim) speaking about the poor conditions of Blacks in America. He attributed their plight to centuries of white oppression. Some of my most vivid teenage memories are of driving through the predominantly white campus of the University of Chicago while playing my then favorite rap groups Public Enemy and N.W.A. Both groups had songs (with names we will not publish) that eloquently stated my feelings about society at that time. So it was very strange that I would eventually find myself in New York attending a predominately white, government-run school (the United States Military Academy at West

Point) and having a short Jewish man as a best friend. God has an interesting sense of humor and a way of crossing the widest of boundaries.

Jesus placed himself in a situation that crossed all of the social and legal customs of the day. In his day Jews and Samaritans did not associate. In fact, Jews held that all Samaritans were "unclean." In John 4 Jesus asked for a drink of water from a Samaritan woman, which is interesting because a Jew would become ceremonially unclean if he even used a drinking vessel handled by a Samaritan. In this case Jesus himself would be separated from the Jewish community until he had performed the necessary purification rites. By his example, Jesus teaches an important lesson about evangelism: Evangelism is about transcending all barriers, whether they be racial, social, gender-based or otherwise.

One of the greatest dangers to our mission of spreading the gospel throughout the world is fear of reaching out to someone different from ourselves. Whether that someone is of a different color, different social status or different ethnic background, we must have the words and example of our Lord deeply rooted in our hearts: "Go and make disciples of *all nations*"—not just white, or just rich, or just blacks, or those around whom we are comfortable, or those who don't intimidate us, or those who seem "open" (Matthew 28:19, emphasis added). Make disciples of "all." All nations are to be saved.

We have all been called to preach. We follow the path forged by the one who transcended all boundaries. Too many of us are sitting in our own little worlds, afraid to reach out to someone different from us. If I have learned anything, it is this: I can preach discipleship until I am blue in the face, but if I do not love other people, *all* people, and share my very life with them, then I have missed the very essence of what it means to be a follower of Christ!

We can spend our lives being intimidated by outward appearances—business suits, flawless diction or job status—instead of seeing people for who and what they are: "harassed and helpless, like sheep without a shepherd" (Matthew 9:36). We must repent of our worldly thinking if we are ever to win the world for Christ. People are people no matter what they look like, where they come from or how successful they may seem. Underneath the most "together" image is a man or woman like any other. Everyone has insecurities, and everyone has flaws. As Paul puts it, "all have sinned and fall short of the glory of God" (Romans 3:23). So why be intimidated? All people struggle with the same issues.

I am grateful today that a little Jewish man (with a big heart) came and shared his life with me while I was busy being Public Enemy Number One. Four years ago, the man who was to become one of my best friends walked into my life. He is white, and I am black (strike one). He is short, and I am tall (strike two). He likes Frank Sinatra, and I like James Brown (strike three). We are about as different as you can get. God does have a sense of humor! I am very grateful for Larry Salberg, because he is my friend—a friend who transcended all barriers to help me know the God he knew. That is what Jesus did; that is what evangelism does!

I know that wherever you live, you are reading this and hoping that your family will come to know the God you now know. You are hoping that God will work miracles.

God does and will, if we just do our part! I'm here doing my part, and I pray that wherever you are, you're doing your part. We're all praying for each other. That is team-work; that is evangelism!

Maybe you're a little tired or hesitant to speak to that "sharp" gentleman next to you on the train. But what if we all get tired or hesitant to speak? Imagine that it is your own mother or father who is calling out for help. Picture your brother or sister standing next to you in line. Would you speak if it were your best friend from high school?

Let's break down the barriers that keep us from shar-ing the faith we profess. Barriers of pride and selfishness, laziness and ingratitude, fear and intimidation, all of which keep people from knowing God! That is someone's father you're helping break free from drug addiction by sharing your faith. That is some child's family you're keeping from experiencing the pain of divorce. That is some mother's son you're keeping from suicide. That is what evangelism is; that is what evangelism does.

How, then, can they call on the one they have not believed in? And how can they believe in the one of whom they have not heard? And how can they hear without someone preaching to them? (Romans 10:14).

My (Michele's) heart is palpitating. I think my friend just might witness a cardiovascular explosion right here in the elevator. We are almost at the ninth floor, and soon my fist will actually have to make enough repetitive con-tact with the apartment door so that she will hear us and answer. Maybe she will not answer at all. Then what will I do? I cannot believe this is happening!

Fifteen minutes ago I was merely stopping to pick up a few dishes from my apartment, and thanks to a slip of the tongue by my doorman, I discover that I am about to meet the woman with whom my husband is having an affair. What will I say? What will she say? What would Jesus say? Or more importantly, what wouldn't Jesus say?

> To this you were called, because Christ suffered for you, leaving you an example, that you should follow in his steps.... When they hurled their insults at him, he did not retaliate; when he suffered, he made no threats. Instead, he entrusted himself to him who judges justly (1 Peter 2:21, 23).

My husband's decision to leave God was hard, but this was positively soap-operatic. I thought this stuff only happened to women with names like Fallon, Crystal or Blair and whose lines came from cleverly plotted scripts and story lines. Never to me! I am a disciple. I am trying to live the right way. Has God forgotten me?

> And we know that in all things God works for the good of those who love him, who have been called according to his purpose (Romans 8:28).

We are at the door. I am knocking. She is coming. I am praying. She is answering. Oh man, the rubber is hitting the road. *God, help me be like Jesus!* "Hi," I said. "I need to pick up a few things."

For the sake of time, paper and more dramatic dialogue, I will cut to the chase. There was not any yelling, screaming, hair pulling or object throwing that day. And the truth be told, I think she was more uncomfortable than I was. She was alone—at least I had a friend with me. I asked her if she lived in Manhattan (one of those "Peter on the Mount of Transfiguration" questions), then the Spirit kicked in, and I asked her to come to church with me some-day. She did not answer, and she did not show up at church the next Sunday.

> Therefore, my dear brothers, stand firm. Let nothing move you. Always give yourself fully to the work of the Lord, be-cause you know that your labor in the Lord is not in vain (1 Corinthians 15:58).

A year and a half later, she was met by two other dis-ciples; and after building a friendship with them (coupled with much persuasion and a guarantee that she would not be met at the door by an angry mob), she came to church, studied the Bible and is now not only my sister in Christ, but a very good friend as well.

Her conversion was truly a "That's so God" event. And all humor aside, only God's love and forgiveness can pull off something like that. However, the key to her conver-sion was not just an invitation to church, it was having close friendships with disciples who served her, loved her, spent lots of time with her and showed her in living color that Jesus' ways are in direct opposition to the ways of the world.

I am afraid too many of us have the false impression that evangelism is defined by an invitation to church, but if I may be so bold, I say "Not!" Evangelism is making disciples and teaching them to obey everything that Jesus commanded (Matthew 28:19). That is the standard Jesus sets in the Bible. He teaches us to "go and bear fruit—fruit that will last" (John 15:16). Yes, we are to sow generously (2 Corinthians 9:6), but that is only just the beginning. Jesus spells it out in John 15:12-13:

> "My command is this: Love each other as I have loved you. Greater love has no one than this, that he lay down his life for his friends."

You cannot make a disciple without making a friend. If I do not convince you of anything else, please be convinced of this: The phrase "friendship evangelism" is redundant. Evangelism is friendship, as defined by Christ.

When Jesus was not alone with his Father, his life was socially abundant and full. If he was not at a dinner, a party or a wedding, he was surrounded by his disciples and their friends. Do our lives reflect the same devotion to people? The world will be won for God one relationship at a time—not one invitation at a time. We can build great relationships by relating to people, their interests, accomplishments and environments.

Here are a few suggestions:

- Theme Parties: We recently had an "iced-coffee house party." We served iced coffee with flavored creams and cookies and cakes. Art students brought portfolios and artwork for an informal critique, and we had a singing performance. It was a huge hit. Whatever you choose, be creative and make it excellent. Have fun!

- Take a class or join a gym: Pottery, stained-glass making, acting, cooking, roller blading, dancing. Find out where the people are and join in!
- Sports activities: Join a football or softball league, or start your own!

At a leadership conference, we were challenged to be personally meeting and studying the Bible with people, not just "ministering." I had not met anyone who had become a disciple in almost a year, so I became desperate to do so after the conference. While it can be just as right to pray to meet someone totally different from yourself, I decided to pray to meet my "twin," someone unmistakably like me. It was a bit scary to be so specific, but "nothing is impossible with God" (Luke 1:37).

When I got back from the conference, I called a woman I had met a few months earlier on the train. Her name was Maria, and she actually lived in my apartment building. We were the same age, from the same state, both went to journalism school and to top it off, she was actually a twin! She was a producer for a network newsmagazine, and we hit it off immediately, but she was very busy. I invited her to parties, movies and even dinner at a New York restaurant called "Twin" (no kidding)! Many times she did not return my telephone calls for days or weeks, but I kept praying for her and decided that unless she told me to shove off, I would keep working on our friendship.

After four months she finally studied the Bible and shortly after became a Christian! God answers specific prayers! A month later her twin sister and husband were baptized. They currently lead the preteen ministry in the Baltimore church and my "twins" are doing great!

God can lead us to someone just like us. He can lead us to someone totally different from us. We just have to be ready to seize any opportunity, including the most unlikely ones. We have to be ready to pray, to befriend, to open our mouths and speak. We will never do anything more important than bring another person to Jesus Christ, but with his help we can do it and then do it again.

Focus Thought

My actions can change someone's eternal destiny today.

13

The Heart of a Servant

KARLA GEHL AND NANON TYGETT

"Whoever wants to become great among you must be your servant, and whoever wants to be first must be your slave—just as the Son of Man did not come to be served, but to serve, and to give his life as a ransom for many."

MATTHEW 20:26-28

Talk about a challenge! Jesus Christ, the Son of God, cocreator of the world, Lord of all, head of God's kingdom, the omniscient, omnipotent, said he came into the world to serve—to be a slave. It is not the path we would have expected the only Son of God to take. He deserved honor, yet he chose to honor everyone above himself. He deserved overwhelming gratitude, yet he chose to lay his life down for ungrateful people. He deserved might and praise and glory, yet he chose servitude. He deserved to be a king, yet he chose to be a slave. The New Testament talks of his selflessness—he was constantly meeting needs—giving, teaching, helping, healing, training, loving, serving. Jesus became a slave in this world so we would not have to be slaves to this world.

This is the man we signed up to follow. This is the man whose life we decided to imitate. We need to constantly ask ourselves how our imitation is going with questions like these: Am I constantly meeting needs—giving, teaching, helping, healing, training, loving, serving? Have I been living daily the humble life of a servant? Is Jesus' standard of servitude the one I am holding myself to? We must remember who is lord of our lives now. We have signed up to carry on his mission: to be a slave in this world so that no one would have to be a slave to this world.

The Motivation of a Servant

Some of you reading this may be feeling challenged after that opening paragraph and seeing Jesus' standard. I was when writing it! But I have to admit, as I was feeling challenged, my mind started to wander back to those late nights, coming home at 2:00 A.M. with a sweat-glistened brow and an exhausted sigh, tired after a day of laying down my life and serving all those people God put in my path—and as my mind defensively glamorized my hours of servitude, I thought of Jesus on the cross. And I shut up. I knew that my life was and is nothing close to his. He served to the point of death, and I was feeling good about a few late nights? Yuck! But I think we often do this. We give in to a "woe-is-me" attitude about serving. Sure, we will serve sometimes, maybe a lot, and that is great! But, we have got to keep our motives in check. In order to really test our level of servitude, we have to look beyond just our actions and look at what God sees. We must look at our hearts.

Our hearts are usually the last place we go when we want to change. We like to get the actions going first, but our hearts are the real targets of Satan. He loves nothing more than to keep us religious on the outside but impure in our hearts. That is how he won the Pharisees. Test your heart when it comes to service. Check the inside of the cup. Examine your motives for serving.

Impure Motives

Our motives can be impure when we are "selfish servers." This is no oxymoron. It happens. We sometimes serve and expect something in return. Or we serve and want recognition even to the point of having attitudes if someone does not give us the thanks we feel we deserve. We have got to check our hearts. Are we serving to receive praise from others or for something we will receive in return? Jesus knows how our hearts and minds work. He knows how much Satan tempts us to want recognition for our servitude. In Matthew 6:1-3 he said,

> "Be careful not to do your 'acts of righteousness' before men, to be seen by them. If you do, you will have no reward from your Father in heaven.
> "So when you give to the needy, do not announce it...as the hypocrites do...to be honored by men. I tell you the truth, they have received their reward in full."

Are you a selective server? Are you quick to serve "leaders," but do not feel the same urgency to serve every person with a need in God's church? Are you selective about which jobs you think are "important" enough for you to spend time on? We have got to remember that, as disciples, our lives have been bought at a very high price: Jesus' blood. That means we owe it to him to serve whenever his Father needs us. We must serve anyone, anywhere, anytime, doing any job!

Gratitude

You may be wondering how in the world you can keep your motives pure. The solution is *gratitude*. The minute we stop remembering where we came from and start being ungrateful, we stop serving with pure hearts. But if we constantly remember the life God has saved us from, we will be continually motivated to do anything to show him our gratitude. Take a minute to remember the life you were living before you were a Christian. We have absolutely no reason to ever be ungrateful. God reached into the world, pulled us out of the muck and set us down in his amazing kingdom. Now that we are here, we have no higher priority than to save. If gratitude is constantly our motivation, we will truly become servants like Jesus was—from the inside out.

Serving the Kingdom and the World

I (Karla) had the amazing privilege of becoming a Christian at the age of seventeen. Six months later, just after my eighteenth birthday, I was asked to lead a Bible discussion group consisting of four women, all between the ages of thirty and thirty-five. Suffice it to say that I learned about God's sense of humor then. I was a bit intimidated. I prayed—a lot—and one night I came across Matthew 20:26 about being a slave to all. I remember reading that scripture and being so relieved. Jesus led by serving! I was not sure about this "leadership" thing, but I knew I could serve. And that is what I did. Now, two years later, I am leading a larger group, and that scripture is still the standard. The only difference is that I have more women to serve.

I truly believe that, whether we are in the full-time ministry or not, as single disciples we have more opportunity and time to serve than anyone in God's family. It is why we are here: to lay down our lives for the lost and for God's people. An amazing servant, Cynthia Powell, best summed it up when she said, "This is not the church of 'what have you done for me lately?'!" If we take care of everyone else's needs God will take care of ours!

Here is a heart test. You may find new ways to serve that you have never thought of as you go along. (Hopefully, the right answers are obvious, but give the answer which is most honest about your character.)

1. You arrive at your Bible discussion group five minutes before it's time to start. The leader is frantically trying to make last-minute preparations and to get the house clean. What is your initial thought?

a.) "This place is a mess! I hope everything gets pulled together before my visitor gets here."

b.) "If I were the leader, I would have had things more organized."

c.) "What can I do to help?"

2. You come home after a long day at work. Your roommates are gone, the house is a mess and the sink is piled with dishes...again. You:

a.) See the opportunity to serve and clean the house, re-solving to speak to your roommates later to get a cleaning plan so you can all be righteous in your household.

b.) Clean the house but make sure to "chalk it up" on your record as another time you served them. Resent your roommates for their lack of discipline.

c.) Do your chores and your dishes, being careful not to wash any of theirs so they will see their mess and be con-victed of their sin.

3. You are asked to teach in the children's ministry for the next six-month term. Your response is:

a.) "Six months—that is a long time to be out of service! I feel a cold coming on."

b.) "I would love to! When do I start?"

c.) "I would, but there is no one else in my ministry group who is wise enough to take care of my visitors."

4. You are involved in studying the Bible with someone; she cancels a study appointment because of illness. You:

a.) Think: "What an excuse! If God were important to her, she would come over anyway. She must not be open."

b.) Think: "Whew! Free time! I can go get that full-body massage I've been wanting."

c.) Take her soup, tea and a copy of *Casablanca*. Offer to do her laundry.

5. You are late for an appointment and running up a flight of stairs. You see a woman struggling to get her baby car-riage up the stairs. You:

a.) Manage to get up enough speed to expertly squeeze by, so as to not lose any time.

b.) Stop, offer to help her up the stairs, and then use the opportunity to invite her to church.

c.) Mumble under your breath and quickly find another route.

6. You notice that a brother is not doing well. You:

a.) Give him a quick hug, tell him that you love him and that you'll be praying for him, as you continue on your way.

b.) Avoid contact with him so as not to get into a lengthy discussion.

c.) Stop what you are doing, and find out what you can do to help.

7. The singles are having a "special event." You:

a.) Offer your help and your suggestions.

b.) Wait for someone to ask you to help, and then get an attitude that you were asked.

c.) Do nothing to help, and then notice everything that goes wrong. Make a mental note about the things that you could have done better.

8. There is a single mom with three children who is consistently late for church. You:

a.) Rebuke her for her lateness.

b.) See if you or someone else can arrange to help her in the mornings.

c.) "There's a single mom who's consistently late to service? I hadn't noticed."

9. There is a physically challenged disciple in your group who needs help with some basic household matters. You:

a.) Reason that it will be good for her to work this out on her own and develop more independent patterns.

b.) Tell yourself that the needs are so obvious that there will be others who know her better who will take care of this.

c.) Talk to some of the people who do know her better and ask how you might be able to help.

10. It is Sunday morning. None of your visitors show up and unfortunately, everyone in your ministry group is in the same boat. During the service you:

a.) Listen to the sermon, and every time the preacher says something challenging, think he is talking to you because, after all, you are a horrible disciple; the rest of the people in your group are horrible disciples; God is not with you, and you may as well stop sharing your faith because no one is ever going to come with you anyway.

b.) Notice the other visitors there, and plan to give to everyone in fellowship. Resolve with your group to get someone there the next week.

c.) Feel fine about yourself, because after all, the person who is supposed to be "leading you" does not have anyone there either.

So, how did you do? What did you learn about your heart? How will you change?

Serving the Children

People were bringing little children to Jesus to have him touch them, but the disciples rebuked them. When Jesus saw this, he was indignant. He said to them,

> "Let the little children come to me, and do not hinder them, for the kingdom of God belongs to such as these. I tell you the truth, anyone who will not receive the kingdom of God like a little child will never enter it." And he took the children in his arms, put his hands on them and blessed them (Mark 10:13-16).

Love God? Love Children

I (Nanon) am struck by how indignant Jesus was about how his disciples regarded the children. Basically, Jesus is saying that a lack of understanding of children is an indication of a deeper heart problem. Here he is telling us that we cannot be his disciples without having a heart to love and to serve the children. Jesus was never too busy to stop and say hello to a child or to find out what was going on in a child's life. So many of us are so busy with our own agenda that we overlook the children. Or, like the disciples with Jesus, we think that there are more important things we have to do, so we push the children aside.

Think about your church. How many of the children know you by name? When was the last time a child ran across the room and threw his or her arms around you because they were so excited to see you? Do you pray for the children? (When we do, we are praying for God's future kingdom.)

A Heart 'Transplant'

Through serving the children we can begin to have their heart. For example, everything to a child is black and white. Is he a good man or a bad man? Humanism often clouds our judgment, but to a child life is simple. Children love unconditionally; they trust; they don't hold a grudge for long and they are forgiving. We need to imitate their hearts! Unless we do, Jesus says that we will not enter the kingdom of heaven.

Serving the Little Ones

A leader recently said, "The children's ministry disciples the church." Much is revealed in our character by the way we respond to serving in the children's ministry. We indicate our spiritual understanding and insight by our response to serving the children. If we are more excited about working hard for something that brings us recognition in the church or a more prominent leadership position, we are shallow. If we skimp on the time we spend preparing for a children's class, we are revealing our true hearts. Every time we encourage a child, teach a great class or build a strong friendship with a young boy or girl, we must understand we are investing in the future of God's kingdom.

Through the prophet Hosea, God laments, "My people are destroyed from lack of knowledge" (Hosea 4:6). Many movements in history have died because the second generation did not have the heart or knowledge of their parents. God commands us not only to teach the children, but to be great examples:

Only be careful, and watch yourselves closely so that you
do not forget the things your eyes have seen or let them
slip from your heart as long as you live. Teach them to your
children and to their children after them (Deuteronomy 4:9).

It is clearly the parents' responsibility to teach and to train
their children. However, there is an old African proverb
that says, "It takes a village to raise a child." (Someone
recently wrote a book with that title!) This is true of the
church: "It takes a church to raise a child." I truly believe
that if Jesus were here today, he would be teaching in the
children's classes. That is his heart.

An anonymous quote sums up what I'm trying to say:

> A hundred years from now it will not matter
> what my bank account was, the sort of house
> I lived in, or the kind of car I drove...but the
> world may be different because I was im-
> portant in the life of a child.

Serving with Joy

"I am the Lord's servant," Mary answered. "May it be to me
as you have said" (Luke 1:38).

Did you ever stop to think that when the angel approached Mary, she was a young single woman? She probably had her life all planned out. She was getting married
to Joseph, would have his children and live a nice comfortable life. Nowhere in this plan was her giving birth to
the Son of God and taking on the responsibilities that went
with that. Mary's choice to do God's will and to serve him

with all of her heart meant that she was putting everything on the line. She was risking her fiancé, her reputation and her life as she knew it. But Mary was willing to risk it all in order to serve God with all of her heart and all of her soul.

On New Year's Eve 1996, I prayed that God would put in my life someone I could pour myself into. I prayed, "God, I have so much love to give; please give me someone to share it with!" Now understand, to me that meant a woman to study the Bible with or a man who would become my husband. But, as we all know, God always answers our prayers, but not always the way we think he will. Little did I know that the answer God had in mind for me was a beautiful ten-year-old girl who had an incredible heart and desperately needed to be loved.

Within the first week of the new year a single mother called me and asked for help with her ten-year-old child. They were having some intense conflicts and, in this case, a break from each other seemed wise. Initially I took the child for a weekend, but after much counseling and advice, it became clear that she would need to live with me for a while. I agreed to this because I wanted to help this family, and I had grown to love the little girl. But in my heart I was not sure I wanted to become a single mom right then. I thought, *I mean, what about* me? *What about my life, my time, my needs, my desires? If I do this, I really will not get married. I did not ask for this! Why* me? *What made God think I could handle this tremendous responsibility? (I wonder if Mary felt this way?) I mean, after all, it was only supposed to be for a weekend!*

I became angry and resentful of this child, of the people around me and of God, but I kept praying about it. The answer to my prayer came one afternoon when I looked over in the seat next to me as I drove her home from school. Listening to the challenges of her day, my eyes filled with tears. I could not imagine life without her! She had become very special to me. I knew then that it did not matter any longer about my life, my time, my needs and my desires. The only thing that mattered was that I help this child make it to heaven and give her the purpose of helping others get there too. Then my life will have made a difference. I focused on Matthew 6:25 and 33:

> "Therefore I tell you, do not worry about your life...But seek first his kingdom and his righteousness, and all these things will be given to you as well."

I had to have faith that if God wanted me to be married, to choreograph shows or to do anything else, having a little girl in my life would not stop that. And if he did not want those things for me, well, to quote Mary (Jesus' mother), "I am the Lord's servant. May it be to me as you have said."

Eventually, it seemed best to all concerned that I keep my new "daughter" and I obtained legal custody. So, at the age of thirty-seven I became the legal guardian of an eleven-year-old girl—the miraculous conception, but not quite the way I pictured it! I am so grateful to God for this precious gift!

Jesus came to lay down his life for us so that we might have life to the full (John 10:10). To serve one another wholeheartedly means that we are willing to lay our lives down for each other (John 15:13). Is it easy? No. Is it always fun? No. Does it mean stretching my heart beyond where it's ever gone before? Yes. But it is amazing how God chooses to bring joy to a servant heart. "My servants will sing out of the joy of their hearts" (Isaiah 65:14). Many times the rewards for serving are unexpected and come years down the road. If my only reward is to go to be with God and to take this child with me, that is good enough for me!

FOCUS THOUGHT

How can I serve with the heart of Jesus today?

14

No Turning Back: Single Parenting

MADALINE M. EVANS

For three months I was learning to be a disciple before I finally decided to get baptized. During those three "practice" months, I never considered the challenge of being a single parent for Christ.

I remember driving one Wednesday night after my baptism from South Orange, New Jersey, to church on 76th Street and Central Park West in Manhattan. It was cold and icy. I got off work on time, picked up my children and headed for the Lincoln Tunnel. My plan was to eat a quick dinner once we got to the city. I started off happy, but the tunnel traffic was making me very late and my two teenage boys' bickering about going to New York three nights a week was giving me a headache. This scene, which seemed to repeat itself every day after I decided to be a disciple, wreaked havoc on my heart and made me not want to do it anymore. It was too hard. By the time I got through that tunnel and found a parking space, church was over. I had no joy, no smile for anyone. I had not fed my children. I missed the whole service. I wanted to shake the kids silly, and I had no kind words for the people who greeted me. The very thing that I practiced for three months was now on the verge of being tossed aside forever, because it was just too hard. On the way home, I remembered a few words of that song we sang all the time "no turning back, no turning back"—and I knew what I needed to do.

Being a single parent and a disciple can be quite challenging and, at times, more difficult than it is for any other group in the church. And yet, I cannot think of a better place for single parents than in God's church because they need the love, encouragement and support that only God's kingdom can provide. That eventful Wednesday night happened to me so that God could remind me of my promise to him—a promise and a decision that we, as single parents, must remember even if we do not remember anything else: "I have decided to follow Jesus, no turning back, no turning back."

It Starts with Me

> Impress them on your children. Talk about them when you sit at home and when you walk along the road, when you lie down and when you get up (Deuteronomy 6:7).

My nest is now empty, but when I became a disciple as a single parent, I knew that, first of all, I had to have my own deep convictions about loving Christ and loving the church deeply. Then and only then would my children not be an excuse. Instead, my children would be what motivated me to be my best. Many different circumstances lead to being a single parent. It does not really matter how it happened, but what does matter is the impact the full-time parent has on the eternal destiny of the children. I wanted to set an example for my children. I wanted them to have plenty of evidence to believe me when I said that Jesus had changed my life. I wanted them to remember how Jesus used my life to positively influence the lives of others. I wanted them to love the church with me.

I knew that the only way to have this kind of impact on my children was to live a life that was committed to Jesus every single day! It started with feeding on God's word daily in the morning before they got up. God wanted me to be equipped for their day and mine. The dailiness of raising them was a big responsibility, and I had to be prepared. I needed God's ammunition. My children needed to see me in my Bible, and they needed to see me on my knees, consistently (Deuteronomy 4:9).

I needed to be excited about getting to service, being in service and being with the family of believers. My children imitated me. If I whined and complained about going to church, so did they. I always tried to find the great things that happened at church, and I talked about them with joy, fondness and appreciation. My children needed to hear these positive statements and they needed to hear them often.

My children also needed to see me fulfilling my God-given purpose in life: I wanted people to know God. My children needed to see it, to hear about it and to know that I loved it. I told them about the women with whom I was studying the Bible. Those same women ate with us, spent the night at our house, went on outings, helped me at home, and generally were with us a lot.

My children also knew who I discipled. They talked with them, laughed with them, and saw them cry when they were hurt. They saw them leave our home encouraged. They saw them come back at the same time every week. They missed them when my discipling partners changed. Overall, I know they saw what a disciple is, and I know they were happy that I was one. Do your children see what a disciple is by looking at you? (2 Timothy 1:5).

It Continues with Them

> Train a child in the way he should go,
>   and when he is old he will not turn from it
>   (Proverbs 22:6).

Being a single parent, I could not use the lame statement (or excuse) of "Boy, wait till your father gets home...," because the mother and father were already home—they were me! If I was upset with my children because of their behavior, if I was troubled by their lack of respect for me, if I was frustrated with their disobedience, if I was hurt by their lack of love—who could I blame? I could blame my discipling partner. I could blame the church leaders. I could blame God. But the truth of the matter was that I had nobody to blame but myself. During those difficult times, my temptations were to close off, shut down or quit, but then I remembered that little song, the one that played endlessly in my head: "no turning back, no turning back." I turned to God, and as always, he gave me the answers.

The first step in discipling our children is to know who they really are. I had to be gut-level honest about who my children were. For one whole week I prayed, observed and took notes on each of them. I watched how they inter-acted with people, how they talked to their peers, how they treated people, how they looked at them, etc. I listened to how they talked on the phone, how they took messages, how they talked to people at church. I listened to and watched how they responded to me: what they said, what they did. As I studied what I had discovered, I was amazed! I did not like what I saw, and I was afraid of the task before me. I wanted to quit before I even started. But I chose prayer and God's word instead.

The next step was to change myself. I realized that I had to respect people before I could teach my children to respect others. I had to obey before I could teach them to obey. I had to be on time, tell them about my whereabouts, let my "yes" be yes, and my "no" be no. I had to put them first as I had promised, stick to our times together, be there for their important moments in life and speak to them with respect, love and encouragement. I had to stop complain-ing, being negative and argumentative. I had to stop feel-ing guilty for being the only parent, which made me spoil them and overgive to compensate for the missing parent. It was time to lead with the authority, love and power God had given me all along (2 Peter 1:3-10).

After I had compiled the long list of things my children needed to change, I sat down with a very special friend, Andee Epstein-Finnerty. At the time she was ten years younger than I, had never been married, had no children, never had a boyfriend and was a Jewish white woman. Our backgrounds were as different as I could imagine! Yet, through her godliness she helped me to fall in love with my children. We selected three areas for each child to work on at a time. She gave me ideas on how to help them change, how to encourage them in their growth, and how not to go on to the next change until we had truly seen a difference. It was challenging, and we ran into many snags, but we kept getting advice from different parents in the church—wise ones, of course!—who had raised faithful, wonderful children. Parents like Les and Jean Johnson, Archer and Jency Taliaferro, and Mike and Brenda Leatherwood provided advice from the Scriptures, and I obeyed it. They laugh when we reminisce about some of the funny things we tried. But God blesses obedience, and he blessed me (Proverbs 12:15, Proverbs 15:22).

Worth All the Effort!

Today my older son is drug-free and loves life. He is not a disciple yet, but he respects me and the church. He knows God spared us, and for that he is truly thankful. I have no doubt that he will become a disciple. My younger son is a disciple who works in the church office ministering to the needs of the New York church's largest super region. He has been leading Bible discussion groups since his second year of college, loves the lost and loves God's church.

The life of a single parent with children is difficult—no doubt about it—but without God, it would be impossible. I'm so grateful I had him with me!

FOCUS THOUGHT

Faith is the victory—in all circumstances.

15

For Your Maker
Is Your Husband:
After Divorce

KAYREN CARTER

Growing up in a traditional church and being taught the basic principles of God, I had deep convictions about marriage. Marriage was a commitment until death. I had no other dream but to marry, have children and stay home to care for them. I knew that was what would make me happy...that was what I wanted for my life.

My dreams came true. I was married and my husband and I were blessed with four incredible children: Elizabeth, Kimberly, Cinnamon and finally our son, Tommy. Those years were the best of times and the worst of times. But through them all I was totally committed to making it work. No matter how difficult things got, divorce was never an option in my heart.

After sixteen years of marriage, I became a disciple, but my husband did not. Then I was even more determined to be the wife and mother God wanted me to be. I spent so much of my time praying and trying to keep my marriage together. One morning as I was reading my Bible, a passage cut through my heart like a sword. In Matthew 22:23-30, the Sadducees were attempting to trap Jesus with a question about marriage: In heaven whose wife would this woman be who had been married seven times? Jesus answered,

> "You are in error because you do not know the Scriptures or the power of God. At the resurrection people will neither marry nor be given in marriage; they will be like the angels in heaven" (Matthew 22:29-30).

I was cut because I saw how much of my life had been spent trying to hold on to my marriage. I decided to trust God and pour my heart into being the best disciple I could be.

I will never forget the day my husband gave me an ultimatum: "If you do not leave 'that church,' I'm leaving you!" I remember my heart stopping for a second, my mind racing through years of marriage. But within a few seconds my answer was, "I will never leave God or his church. Where else could I go?" About six months later he took me to dinner at our favorite spot and told me he was leaving me. That was December 9 and on December 29 he had divorce papers delivered to my front door. MERRY Christmas...!

"Divorce"—to me a word that was worse than cancer or leprosy, a fate worse than death! I thought, *No!!!!! I just will not let him do it. I will not sign anything. No! I will not be divorced!* Clyde and Jane Whitworth, my good friends and leaders in the church, sat me down in their family room in Atlanta and read me 1 Corinthians 7:15, "But if the unbeliever leaves, let him do so. A believing man or woman is not bound in such circumstances." The Scriptures spoke, and I yielded.

We had been married for twenty-six years. The long process of accepting and dealing with reality began. I was an incurable dreamer. I had always believed that I would one day be an elder's wife, or that my husband and I would lead a church together. But the reality was that I was divorced, and worse still a *single mom*—horror of horrors—or so I thought.

In the beginning, day and night ran together. It all seemed black. I spent hours flat on the floor of my bathroom (don't feel too sorry for me—it was big and carpeted!) praying and crying out to God to save me from death. And I was heard because of surrendering to God one day at a time (Hebrews 5:7). Only the Sovereign Lord can heal that kind of pain. I cried, and I prayed. I prayed, and I cried.

Prayer was the beginning of healing, but without my relationships in the kingdom I would have miserably failed. It was so wonderful to have sisters to confide in and to be totally gut-wrenchingly honest with. There was nothing I kept to myself or from God—not the pain, not the sinful thoughts.

On our twenty-fifth anniversary the previous year, I had had a "boudoir" portrait done as a gift to my husband. It was tasteful—don't struggle—and he loved it. Now what was I supposed to do with it?! I was *so* tempted to wrap it in brown paper and send it as a Christmas present to him and his new wife! My sisters of course advised me against this and helped to keep me from so much sin! They let me talk; they let me cry and cry and cry. Then they would remind me of my loving, compassionate and sovereign God. Thank goodness for Jane Whitworth, Carolyn Massengil, Anita Banadyga and many others. Several times I flew all the way to New York City to spend time with Anita for help and encouragement. This is how I survived: prayer, relationships and scriptures like the following:

> The LORD is with me; I will not be afraid.
>   What can man do to me?...
> The LORD is my strength and my song...
> I will not die but live,
>   and will proclaim what the LORD has done
> (Psalm 118:6, 14, 17).

> I love you, O LORD, my strength.
> The Lord is my rock, my fortress, and my deliverer;
>   my God is my rock, in whom I take refuge....
> In my distress I called to the Lord;
>   I cried to my God for help....
> ...he heard my voice...
> He reached down from on high and took hold of me;
>   he drew me out of deep waters....
> He brought me out into a spacious place;
>   he rescued me because he delighted in me....
>   ...my God turns my darkness into light....
> Therefore I will praise you among the nations, O LORD
> (Psalm 18, excerpts).

This psalm became my psalm. Thank goodness for my purpose to "praise [God] among the nations," to seek and to save the lost. It saved my life because it took my focus off myself! One day in an encouraging letter, my daughter Kimberly sent me a scripture, Isaiah 54:5, which became my theme: "For your Maker is your husband—the LORD Almighty is his name."

In the end God put my life back together, and like Job, the Lord has blessed the latter part of my life more than the first (Job 42:12). I was determined to persevere and to do radical things to forge my new life as a single mom.

That first year following my divorce, I took Cinnamon and Tommy, my teens still at home, on two life-changing trips. We went to London, England, to an International Teen Conference where they spent a week with teens from all over the world. I became a teen myself and participated in the entire conference! Then the three of us also went to Cape Town, South Africa, to help start the church with Steve and Lisa Johnson and Buzz and Anita Banadyga. It was a trip that changed all of our lives and gave us a new perspective and dream for the worldwide kingdom of God.

Being a single mom was a challenge. I began to lead the single moms' ministry in the Atlanta church. I gutted it out in the beginning and then learned to love it. I experienced the reality of Mark 10:29-30:

> "I tell you the truth," Jesus replied, "no one who has left home or brothers or sisters or mother or father or children or fields for me and the gospel will fail to receive a hundred times as much in this present age."

My children have had many moms and dads in the kingdom. In every situation I had many mothers and fathers to help me work things out. It gave me so much confidence, so much hope.

As for me, God had given me "myself" back. Through the years, I had lost myself in a very overly dependent relationship. (Some even described it as an "addictive" relationship.) I had thought that I was nothing without him, that I could not survive without him in my life. I really thought life would be over without him. God gave me back my childlike heart that knew that I could do anything that I set my mind to do. I regained my confidence, spunkiness, courage and my self-esteem. I began to like myself again. I even ride roller coasters now though I was afraid of them as a child! I can watch movies like *Braveheart* and walk out feeling brave! I remember the day when Jane Whitworth told me that I was like a bird set free from its cage. God has truly worked miracles in my heart and character, and today I am totally secure with him.

In 1992 Lisa Johnson came to Atlanta, Georgia, and asked for Cinnamon to come to New York City (at only seventeen years of age!) to go to college and train with her in the ministry. One year later the Johnsons asked me to move to New York to go into the full-time ministry. I was fifty years old, so I can testify that it is never too late! It has been four of the best years of my life.

In October of 1995, I was appointed a women's ministry leader. I have had many responsibilities—I have even led the women in a whole sector of the church—but now I am realizing a dream come true. I am at my daughter Cinnamon's side, helping her with the daytime ministry and the NYU campus ministry. Cinnamon and her husband, Dan Conner, lead the Manhattan Super Region of the New York City Church of Christ. She just celebrated her twenty-third birthday. I am also working side by side with Rachel Hirschfeld to convert "not a few" prominent women in this great city of New York.

My daughter Kimberly and her husband, Robert Duncan,—the "Radical Lovers"—lead the music ministry in the Boston church. And now another dream has come true: My daughter Elizabeth and her husband, David, and their children have moved to New York City to be a part of the church here. My son, Tommy, who has been at the University of Georgia the past two years, has just moved here to New York City to finish school and be with the church also. God has truly blessed my life more than I could have ever dreamed. I tell God daily that I refuse to go through the "pearly gates" without all my children, and my God answers my prayers! He is truly the Sovereign Lord:

> For you, O God, tested us;
>   you refined us like silver.
> You brought us into prison
>   and laid burdens on our backs.
> You let men ride over our heads;
>   we went through fire and water,
>   but you brought us to a place of abundance
>   (Psalm 66:10-12).

FOCUS THOUGHT

God has plans to prosper me
more than I can ever ask or imagine.

16

Facing the Future: Faith or Doubt?

MADALINE M. EVANS

"...For I know the plans I have for you," declares the LORD, "plans to prosper you and not to harm you, plans to give you hope and a future."

JEREMIAH 29:11

About one month after I became a disciple, I remember crying my heart out for three consecutive Sunday sermons—during the entire sermon! People would gather around me and try with everything they had to console me but to no avail. I knew I was struggling with being overwhelmed. I was overwhelmed by the reality of my life: being in the church, having my career and being a single mom, along with this disciple thing I had taken on. These things were also known as "my future." *Where was all of this taking me?*

I was overwhelmed because I was afraid. All I knew was that I was not happy where I was. I was single, and I wanted desperately to be married, but there were very few men in the church at that time. (I became the eighty-fourth member of the New York City church when I was baptized.) As a thirty-two year old, black, single mom and a high-powered, opinionated, independent executive, I thought, *Who wants to take on that burden? Who would want to be bothered with all that?* I was also concerned about my career: *How could I continue to be successful if I was always going to church and trying to get others to go with me?* I viewed it as a lot of work, and it seemed so hopeless. All I could do was cry! I had succeeded in exasperating myself. I was struggling with my perception of my future, and the bottom line was that I was faithless. I had to decide something. I could not keep crying during every sermon! I had to decide how I was going to face my future in the kingdom of God—with faith or with doubt.

My God Is So Big, So Strong and So Mighty

As for God, his way is perfect...
It is God who arms me with strength
        and makes my way perfect (Psalm 18:30, 32).

We need to remember that God is greater than we and live like it! This is God's kingdom, his church. His Son died for the sins of the world, and his Spirit lives in all his disciples. His plan is perfect. When I finally came to grips with that, I stopped crying.

When we think about what God does to make us great for his kingdom, we have to realize that we really cannot lose! We have to stop crying and get up and take on the task God puts before our eyes at every moment, whatever it may be. For me it was simply finding someone to study the Bible with. I decided to talk to everyone in my path, and God blessed it! Then God started to give me more responsibilities like teaching other disciples how to be effective, using my home to have discussion groups and using my car to help people get to New York. And God blessed it! After that it was leading a Bible discussion group, being in a discipleship group with leaders, and speaking at workshops. And God blessed it.

Over the years, God's plan for me has included working in the church office, training church administrators all over the world and serving as controller and board secretary for one of the largest churches in the movement. And God continues to bless it!

Am I married yet? No, but I am faithful and very happy. Have I grown in my career? Absolutely! Do I struggle with discouragement about my future? Not any more! God has carved out all of our futures. We just have to use everything he gives us to be everything we can for him, immediately. I was crying because I was fighting God, and fighting God hurts. It was time to surrender my "wants" in exchange for his "future."

You Deserve a 'Life' Today!

I was born very poor, and grew up with no father and an alcoholic mother. In my senior year of high school, I had my first child. I had won a full four-year scholarship to the school of my choice. During my freshman year of college I had my second child. I graduated on time and worked for some of the best corporations in America. Before I became a disciple, I was well educated, financially secure, successful, lonely, afraid and mad at the world.

Today, my life is a testimony to God and to his glory. I love my life! I am grateful for what God planned for me.

He opened doors that I know I had nothing to do with, all because he loved me. He set me up to win despite the adversity in my life. We all have a past and a story to tell, no matter who we are. But wherever we are right now, if we are in God's church, we have a fantastic plan already set for us. We have to "just do it"!

> "In the same way, let your light shine before men, that they may see your good deeds and praise your Father in heaven" (Matthew 5:16).

> "This is to my Father's glory, that you bear much fruit, showing yourselves to be my disciples" (John 15:8).

We each need to look honestly at our lives and assess where we are. Is God being glorified? Would people be impressed? Are you impressed? I would try picking one thing that you would like to let God be glorified in. Is it your bad roommate situation, your sloppy apartment, your unhappiness with your finances, your difficulty with weight, your poor job performance? Decide today. Get with a friend, someone who would love to see you be your best for God and take their advice. Then take one step toward the goal. Pray, and let God do the rest. He blesses hard work, pure hearts and obedience (Matthew 5:3-10).

I am reminded of so many disciples whose lives changed significantly because they decided to let God glorify one aspect of their lives. i think about Maria Rodriguez, who always wanted a high school diploma but was afraid and lacked confidence to carry it out. After much prayer, tears and gut-level openness, she decided to just see who offered GED programs. This led to filling out applications just for fun, which eventually led to a GED less than a year later. Just think: She overcame her biggest fear and accomplished her heart's desire in less than a year! Not to mention that she now has a boyfriend, has passed her driving test, takes part-time college classes and most importantly, has led many people to Christ.

Or consider Sherry Miller, who had an MBA but no job, no driver's license and lived out of a suitcase. Sherry was an awesome sister who was quite fruitful, but the bottom line was that she did not have a life. Through much coaching and great humbling by God and a good friend, Sherry decided to get her driver's license. This led to her buying a car, and when the other single sisters saw what Sherry did, they followed suit. As a result, six other singles in our suburban ministry got cars in less than a month. You can imagine how God was glorified with that many cars for the kingdom! Sherry is now the controller for a booming pediatric practice in our area that is staffed totally by disciples. She also designed a computer training workshop and trained our single moms in Harlem, using Columbia University's computer lab for free. And all this at her own initiative.

> The LORD will fulfill his purpose for me;
>   your love, O LORD, endures forever—
>   do not abandon the works of your hands (Psalm 138:8).

There are countless other stories I could share. We have to stop crying and whining and complaining. We have to decide to get a life. God has given each of us many talents. We need to pray that he will show us how to use them,

one at a time, until his glory radiates throughout our lives!
I believe God had my entire future mapped out way before
I even had a clue. And now that I have caught up with his
vision, I would not change it for the world! I believe this
same truth exists for everyone in God's kingdom. Decide
today to face the future with faith.

FOCUS THOUGHT

The One who holds the future holds me.

Never Quit

G. STEVE KINNARD

One day in first-century Palestine, a scribe sat back to listen to a rabbi from Nazareth named Jesus answer some questions posed to him by religious leaders of the various Jewish sects. The Pharisees and a political sect called the Herodians asked Jesus if it was proper to pay taxes to Caesar or not. Jesus answered them, "Give to Caesar what is Caesar's, and to God what is God's" (Matthew 22:21). The Pharisees and Herodians marveled at his answer.

Next a Sadducee stepped up to ask Jesus the question that had baffled many great teachers, especially those of the Pharisee sect. They asked, in essence, "If a woman marries seven times and all of her husbands die, who will be her husband in heaven?" Seven marriages, seven dead husbands—was this the black-widow spider syndrome?

Jesus answered by saying, "You are in error because you do not know the Scriptures or the power of God" (Matthew 22:29). The Sadducee dared not ask another question.

The scribe had taken all of this in. Maybe this Jesus could answer the question that he had longed to have answered for so many years: Could the entire law of Moses be encapsulated in one commandment? Of the 613 individual laws of the Pentateuch—365 "do not's" and 248 "do's"—which one is most important? So he asked Jesus, "Teacher, which is the greatest commandment in the Law?" (Matthew 22:36).

Jesus answered by reciting the Shema Yisrael from Deuteronomy 6:4-5 which every Jew was to recite twice daily: "Hear, Israel, the Lord your God is one, and you will love the Lord your God with all of your heart, all of your soul, and all of your mind, and all of your strength." But then Jesus added, "The second is this: 'Love your neighbor as yourself'"(Mark 12:29-31, author's translation).

Jesus answered the scribe by giving him the essence of his message. Those who do these two things will find everything else. These two commandments sum up all we are trying to say in this book

Once you start on this journey of learning to love God with all your heart, soul, mind and strength, you must be determined to never give up on God. As a single disciple you will have many temptations thrown your way—job offers, worldly relationships, material desires, recreational distractions. The world paints the single life as the time to "sow your wild oats," to "experience life," and to "do all the things you won't be able to do when you're married with children." Thus the temptations for the single may be different than those of the married person. The married person might plow through a tough time spiritually by saying, "I've got to make it through this time for my marriage/my children." The single without kids cannot say that. He must push through the dark times without these motivations. He must fully comprehend the essence of Christianity—to love the Lord your God with all your heart, soul, mind and strength. It is important to decide when the journey is started that you will not give up.

Can you picture yourself as a zealous disciple when you are fifty, sixty, seventy years old? Can you see yourself living faithfully for the Lord on into the twenty-first century? To love God with all your heart, soul, mind and strength means you will love him with your all today, tomorrow, a year from now, and two decades from now. Never quit!

I'm reminded of a story I heard once:

A duck walked into a bar and asked for an orange. The bartender replied, "I don't carry oranges." The duck left.

The next day the duck walked into the same bar and asked for an orange. The bartender again said he had no oranges. The duck left.

The third day the duck walked into the bar again and asked for an orange. This time the bartender was livid. He shouted, "For three days, Mr. Duck, you have waddled into my bar and asked for an orange! For three days I have told you that I have no oranges! I do not have, will not have, will never get any oranges! If you come in here tomorrow and ask for an orange, I am going to nail your webbed feet to my wall! Now, get out!" The duck left.

The next day the duck waddled into the bar, looked up at the bartender and asked, "Do you have any nails?"

The bartender replied, "No."

The duck responded, "Then do you have any oranges?"

What is the moral? For our purposes, it is don't be a quitter. Keep coming back. Be determined. With God's help, figure out a way to stay on the road. Be resourceful, prayerful, and humble, but love the Lord your God with all your heart, soul, mind and strength, and love your neighbor as yourself. Do it today, tomorrow, two years from now, two decades from now. Never quit. This is the essence of Christianity and this is the path to life.

Contributors

All contributors are on the staff of the New York City Church of Christ.

GARY BARBER holds a degree in design and has been a disciple since 1993. He leads the ministry to professionals in Manhattan.

JIM BROWN, evangelist and leader of the northern ministries of the NYC church, holds a degree in business finance and has been a disciple since 1981. He and his wife, Teresa (below), have two children: daughter Mackenzie and son Dylan.

TERESA DAVIS BROWN holds a degree in English and is the women's ministry leader in the northern ministries of the NYC church.

KAYREN CARTER became a disciple in 1978. She has six grandchildren and is a women's ministry leader in the Daytime Ministry in Manhattan.

DANIEL CONNER, JR. is an evangelist and the leader of all the Manhattan ministries. He holds degrees in English and American literature and has been a disciple since 1993. Dan and Cinnamon (below) were married in the Spring of '97.

CINNAMON CONNER, women's ministry leader of all the Manhattan ministries, became a disciple as a teenager.

JODI DOUGLAS became a disciple in 1992, earning a degree in English while interning in the campus and singles ministries of the NYC church. She was appointed a women's ministry leader in 1995 and currently coleads the arts ministry in Manhattan.

MADALINE M. EVANS, controller and regional financial administrator for the NYC church, has her degree in accounting and is a CPA. She has been a disciple since 1984.

KARLA GEHL moved to New York to pursue a career as an opera singer and became a disciple at 17. Six months later she went into the full-time ministry and became a women's ministry leader at 19. She currently leads the women in a Manhattan ministry.

T.S. GRANT trained in the US Air Force as a law-enforcement officer and specialized in K-9 patrol, narcotics and explosives detection. After moving to NYC in pursuit of an entertainment career, he became a disciple in 1992. He currently leads the Westside Ministry in Manhattan.

MARSHA HYMAN, a disciple since 1992, holds degrees in psychology and counselor education. She is now coleading the Media Ministry in Manhattan.

G. STEVE KINNARD is an evangelist and teacher in the New York City Church of Christ and a doctoral candidate at Drew University. Author of *The Call of the Wise,* he and his wife, Leigh, have two children: Chelsea and David.

ANNA LEATHERWOOD was appointed a women's ministry leader in 1994 while still a teenager. She attended New York University and presently leads the women in the campus sector at NYU.

JAMES W. MCPHERSON, evangelist and leader of the ministry in Harlem, holds degrees in systems engineering and business administration from the US Military Academy (West Point) and has been a disciple since 1992.

REBECCA OKONKWO holds a degree in business administration and is the women's ministry leader for the Washington Heights ministry. She has been a disciple since 1989.

AUGUSTIN RODRIGUEZ leads the Daytime Ministry in Manhattan and has been a disciple since 1994. He holds a degree in media arts, with a major in illustration, and has worked as a professional actor.

MICHAEL A. SAGE holds a degree in fine arts and has been a disciple since 1994. He currently leads the Media Ministry of the NYC church.

STEVE TETRAULT, evangelist and leader of the Eastside Manhattan ministry, has been a disciple since 1991. He holds degrees in graphic design and advertising design and has been married since 1994. He and his wife, Tricia, have one daughter: Nicole.

NANON TYGETT has been a disciple since 1990 and holds a degree in fine arts. She now works full time in the children's ministry of the NYC church.

MICHELE VAUGHN holds degrees in journalism and accessory design and has been a disciple since 1991. She currently coleads the ministry to professionals in Manhattan and is also the owner of and designer for Michele Vaughn Creations, a line of baby shoes and hats.

GARRY W. VERMAAS holds advanced degrees in civil engineering and has coauthored several internationally published papers. Presently, he is a minister in the Arts Ministry of the NYC church, an adjunct professor of engineering at the University of Connecticut, and a doctoral candidate in civil engineering at Columbia University.

KEISHA WILLIAMS attended the American Musical and Dramatic Academy and has been a disciple since 1993. She is now a women's ministry leader in Manhattan.

Other Books from Discipleship Publications International

9 to 5 and Spiritually Alive
A book for Christian women in the workforce
by Sheila Jones

Victory of Surrender
An in-depth study of a powerful biblical concept
by Gordon Ferguson

Mind Change: The Overcomer's Handbook
*For anyone who needs to overcome
any difficulty or challenge in life*
by Tom Jones

Discipling
*A comprehensive teaching about
God's plan to train and transform his people*
by Gordon Ferguson

The Killer Within
*A riveting comparison of several
African diseases to the sin in our hearts and lives*
by Mike Taliaferro

Audio Products from Discipleship Publications International

Dating in the Kingdom
Biblical and practical help
from first date to going steady
by Jim and Theresa Brown

Working 9 to 5
Encouragement and input for
Christian working women
by Madaline Evans, Debby Miller,
Sheila Jones and Kim Walters

Real God—Real Men
Lessons from Genesis for men
by Sam Laing

Real God—Real Women
Lessons from Genesis for women
by Kay McKean

Walking with God
Developing a dynamic walk with God
by Russ Ewell

Out of the Pit
Healing the scars of the past
and learning a new way of thinking
by Dr. Hardy Tillman

More Than Conquerors
Breaking the bonds of the past
and becoming all God meant for us to be
by Dr. Hardy Tillman

Draw Near to God
Growing closer to God as we grow
older in our faith
by Gordon Ferguson

For information about ordering
these and many other resources from DPI,
call
1-888-DPI-BOOK
or from outside the U.S.
617-938-7396.

World Wide Web
http://www.dpibooks.com

Who Are We?

Discipleship Publications International (DPI) began publishing in 1993. We are a non-profit Christian publisher
committed to publishing and distributing materials that
honor God, lift up Jesus Christ, and show how his message
practically applies to all areas of life. We have a deep conviction that no one changes life like Jesus and that the
implementation of his teaching will revolutionize any life,
any marriage, any family, and any singles household.

Since our beginning we have published more than 60
titles; plus we have produced a number of important, spiritual audio products. Almost one million volumes have been
printed and our works have been translated into more than
a dozen languages—international is not just a part of our
name. Our books are shipped monthly to every inhabited
continent.

If you would like to receive a complete catalog of our
works, you can call toll free in the U.S., 1-888-DPI-BOOK.
You can order other books listed on the previous pages by
calling the same number 24 hours per day. From outside
the U.S., call 781-937-3883, ext. 231 during Boston-area
business hours.

We appreciate the hundreds of comments we have received from readers. We would love to hear from you. Here
are other ways to get in touch:

Mail: DPI, One Merrill St., Woburn, MA 01801
E-mail: dpibooks@icoc.org